Somebody Tell the Truth

...about being a pastor's wife

Elisa Veal

Somebody Tell the Truth...about being a pastor's wife

Copyright © 2018 - Elisa Veal

ISBN: 97-80999337622 (eBook)

ISBN: 97-80999337639 (Paperback)

Interior Design by: Rik (www.WildSeasFormatting.com)

Cover Design by: Ian J. Miller

Photography by: Walter Williams

Printed in the United States of America

First Edition

Unless otherwise indicated, all Scripture is taken from the King James Version (KJV). Public Domain.

CONTENTS

CHAPTER THREE

CHAPTER FOUR

CHAPTER FIVE

INTRODUCTION

Hello! Allow me to introduce myself. My name is Elisa Veal, and I'm a pastor's wife. What should you call me? Well, this is where the problem begins; my preference is that you call me Elisa. In my church, this is not appropriate. We do not address each other without including a title before our birth names. My husband, the pastor, would prefer that you address me as Pastor Veal, acknowledging my leadership role in the ministry. Most prefer to call me "First Lady" or Lady Veal.

Over the years, I have had to come to terms with being addressed as First Lady. It is very common in African-American churches to address the pastor's wife as such. I've accepted it, but I don't like it. Never have. I was aware that the wives of many politicians bear the same title, it seemed peculiar to me to refer to the pastor's wife in a similar fashion. This concept was particularly alien to me as I didn't grow up attending church. I've often wondered why the church needs to be so formal. I'm not big on titles; personally, I feel it doesn't add to or take away from who I am.

In the church world at large, the title "First Lady" is a big deal. For those raised in ministry, the First Lady is often the highest-ranking female in the church. "Esteem and honor" are words often included when referring to her. She is placed on a pedestal and made to be on display for all to see. When the members are not in church, they can slip easily back into their lives. Yet the First Lady is known around town and must wear her mantle at all times. Most people aren't able to get close enough to her to actually see behind the veneer of her position, and to experience her as the woman she truly is. "Guarded and restrained" are words that I use to describe her. She is an enigma to many, misunderstood and maligned by most.

So, how do I wish to be addressed? I've determined that it really doesn't matter. You choose. I want you to get to know me as the person I really am. I want you to feel comfortable relating to me without titles or nomenclature getting in the way. I am comfortable now with where God has placed me, and if you need to call me First Lady, Sister, Elect Lady, Mother, Elisa or Mrs. Veal, I will respond. I've now learned that what you call me does not matter; it's far more important to be concerned with what God calls us.

Now that we are formally introduced, I would like to formally say "welcome". This book is written for the pastor's wife, you, alone, are my sole audience. If you are reading this book and you are not a pastor's wife, you may want to stop right here.

There may be some information in this book that may apply to the wives of ministerial leaders or even women in ministry, but I have specifically targeted the pastor's wife.

I've found this role to be based in a lonely, desolate place where we are often overlooked and overburdened. So, pastor's wife: this one is for you. In this book you are the star, the main event. You don't have to compete or contend with others. I offer these words to you in a way that I hope will be enlightening and encouraging. This is not a shortcut or Cliff Notes version of how to be a pastor's wife. Nor is this a book of tell-all slander to use as a weapon against another woman. And, most certainly, this is not a revealing, confessional essay to use as an analysis to see what makes her tick.

Instead, what you are holding in your hands was birthed from my "murmuring-complaining-griping-whining-disgruntled-stiff-necked-temper-tantrum-bewildering-isolating-con-founding-wanna-quit-transformative" experience as the pastor's wife. My aim is to take off my shiny, sparkly church lady hat and share with you some of the mishaps, pitfalls, and lessons that I've experienced during my time in ministry.

I want to help you understand that you are not alone. I want to support you through the realization that you can do this. In no capacity am I an authority on this subject; I only speak from my personal views and experiences. These are my opinions, and I offer them to you in the hope that they will assist and provide a bit of transparency concerning what it takes to be the wife of a pastor. Feel free to take what you need to compare and contrast it with your own experiences. This can be a difficult journey, and I would suggest approaching it with trepidation. But you can do it. You really can. I believe in you because I've been and still walk in your very shoes.

CHAPTER

ONE

The First Lady

First of all, I've never encountered a proper explanation as to why we use the term First Lady in the church. How did this title, which was originally used for a politician's wife, get schlepped into ministry? I once heard a story that it was used because pastors were involved with so many different women that his wife was called First Lady to designate that she was above all others.

I have serious doubts about the accuracy of this explanation, and my research has yielded very little information. So, here's my thought: I believe that many years ago, a pastor decided that his wife was on par with those wives of the political elect and chose to "bless" her with a new designation and because the pastor authorized it, everyone else ran with it. Considering that it only takes one "peacock" spirit to start a trend in the church, the dispensation of the title 'First Lady' became part of our church history, doctrine, and culture. So much so that if you try to get people out of the habit of using that title, they refuse to do so. I've had people apologize to me because they've forgotten to call me First Lady.

My experience with this term in the church has often been negative. So negative, in fact, that when I first became a pastor's wife, I shunned the title of First Lady. I forbade people from addressing me as such. You could mispronounce my first name without measure, but under no certain terms were you ever to refer to me as First Lady. I would actually make a face of disgust!

I've found that with the use of this title comes arrogance. The First Ladies in the church are better than all the rest of us women. You aren't allowed to sit in her seat. You have to serve her water. You must cater to her every need. She must automatically be respected as the pastor's wife regardless of whether she deserves it or not.

We jump to please her and make her happy. The title alone mandates that she is above every other woman in the ministry. When she is introduced, there's a deliberate pause after saying her title. This ensures the hearer understands exactly who this woman is and reveres her as thus stated. It aligns her position with the same regard we reserve for the wives of the political elite.

When First Lady shakes your hand, she often extends a limp

hand and a phony smile, while simultaneously scrutinizing your appearance. She is the mean, evil, uppity woman with the big hats and alligator shoes whose arrogance is stronger than her cheap perfume. She is the one who yells the loudest, the first one to do the holy dance and knock over chairs and, oftentimes, the last one who exhibits compassion. She is not me.

I have seen so many First Ladies behaving poorly that they outweigh those who do good. The title itself seems to enable the woman to transcend from the submissive helpmeet as the Bible describes to a domineering prima donna that most women of the church struggle to build a relationship with.

I can, however, understand why the First Lady behaves this way. For all the shortcomings in her life, being a pastor's wife is the closest she will ever come to having celebrity status. To all of those who've talked about her and mistreated her in the past, she says, "Look at me now! I sit in the best seat, and I'm the trophy wife of your esteemed leader." She receives honor because the pastor tells the congregants not to dishonor his wife. She is given respect because the pastor demands that they respect her.

Arrogance has no place in God's house. You make the title; the title should not make you. I believe that Christians should display the characteristics of Jesus in everything they do. Jesus was notable for humility. I use this as a barometer when I meet anyone who calls themselves Christian. My Jesus is humble, and if I can't see that characteristic in you, then I have a hard time believing that you are truly "walking in the Spirit".

Besides, why do we have to have a title anyway? What's wrong with just being the pastor's wife?

Somebody tell the truth! Let's start with me...

Before I begin to ask for the truth from others, let me share my story. When my husband told me that God called him to pastor many years ago, I was not a happy camper. As I alluded to earlier, I was a person who did not attend church as a child, and the idea of Jesus was as foreign to me as hieroglyphics. My only experience had been a handful of times when I'd been dragged to church, and I felt that Christianity was for religious zealots. I was certainly not one of those and had no intention of ever becoming one. I had no appreciation or understanding of the things of God, and I thought they were restrictive, boring, and archaic.

I felt as if I'd received the equivalent of a sucker punch. This was not what I had signed up for when I said the words "I do".

We were supposed to be a stylish, carefree young couple, and that did not equate with Christianity in my book. My opinion was that the monotony and restriction of a Christian lifestyle would destroy who I was as a person. Furthermore, the types of individuals whom I'd previously encountered in the church, including the various pastors' wives, only confirmed my negative thoughts. I felt they were shallow, fake and domineering.

This did not give me much hope. I struggled at first, a lot. Fast forward several years later to me dragging my feet along my Christian journey, I finally got to a point where I could actually sit through a church service and pay attention the entire time. Much to my astonishment, I had gained a level of proficiency with the King James version of the Bible and felt like I was beginning to understand things. It was at this point my husband declared, "Now, it's time." God was telling him to start the ministry.

Aargh! *So, now, I have to be a pastor's wife? I've just gotten comfortable being a Christian.* No more Sister Veal; it was now First Lady Veal. I wasn't ready for that transformation, nor had I ever felt so inadequate and unqualified in my life. I had no idea as to what to do. Over the years I'd witnessed lots of incorrect and inappropriate behaviors and knew what not to do, but at a complete loss as to what I should be doing.

I wanted to quit everything. I wanted to leave both ministry and my marriage. My desire was to be a fashionable, continental type of woman. Not an old stodgy pastor's wife or a fake plastic First Lady. At that time, I blamed God. My husband had been transformed into another man, and our lives began to move down an uncertain path and it scared me. I was dreading the launch of the ministry.

In the beginning

I often compare the birthing of the ministry within our husbands to the childbearing process a wife experiences. God has planted the vision for the ministry in your husband just as a baby is implanted in you. It is often an intimate and deeply moving experience that does not initially include you. The vision will grow and mature within your husband and cause symptoms to manifest, like what a woman experiences as the baby grows within her body. Just as you become excited with great anticipation for the new arrival; so, will he concerning ministry. As your focus and conversation will involve the upcoming birth, understand that this is what your husband may solely focus on. As you had help with the labor and delivery of your baby, you will now be called upon to help your husband as he labors and delivers this ministry into the earthly realm. You will be the midwife in this process. It doesn't stop there!

As with the birth of a baby, constant care is required for a new ministry. There will be late, sleepless nights, walking the floor, caretaking, etc. I hope you understand where I'm going with this. We cannot resent, rebel, or shut down when our husband's time is consumed and engulfed in ministry. Imagine how you'd react if you were left alone to care for a newborn baby. You must understand the position your spouse is in during this time and fulfill your role.

The Bible asks: Can two walk together, except they be agreed? (Amos 3:3). Your position is vital; don't undervalue what you are called to do during this time. Don't underestimate how your lack of involvement throughout this period could undermine the success of the ministry.

Your life is about to change. You must learn to welcome it. Grab your Bible, put on your seatbelt, and prepare for the ride of your life as you begin to see things in an entirely new perspective. Being in ministry is much like surfing because there's a huge wave coming your way. Fearlessly, you must jump on that board, learn to balance, have no fear and surf that wave or prepare to get beaten, battered and tossed.

As a pastor's wife (PW), the first thing you'll need to do is take care of your husband, the pastor. Your job is to meet his needs. Your second job is to be the first member of the church. You must exhibit exemplary behavior; you must be praying, worshipping, and fasting. It is imperative that you keep growing spiritually. You must be prepared for the attacks of the enemy. You may be called to wear many hats in the ministry; be ye always ready. Over the years, I've had to teach, preach, sing, administrate, facilitate, counsel, and more!

As the ministry increases, you will be called to increase. Don't worry; God has already prepared you for whatever He calls you to do. Just have a willing heart, and He will provide instruction. At times, it may be on-the-job training, but have faith; instruction will come.

The enemy will come too, in ways expected and unexpected. Be prepared to weather the storm and be an unwavering support to your husband. There may be times when the enemy will try to discredit your husband. You must be at his side, praying, supporting, and worshipping God. You are to be the stability he needs, enduring difficulties and maintaining a brave face for the world.

The vision

God has given your husband, the pastor, a vision for the ministry he is starting. He has downloaded plans and directives that need to be established in the earthly realm for such a time as this. You are called to be the help concerning this work. God will seldom share the vision with you. Don't get mad, instead, get an understanding. You're going to need to come into agreement with what God has given your husband. This is not an opportunity to launch your own vision or to subvert what God has established. You must help your husband.

It is imperative that you learn and understand this vision. You must be able to speak articulately about it and submit fully to it. There must be a complete and total agreement before the launch of the ministry. If there are any areas where you are struggling as a PW, you must pray and speak with your husband concerning the things that are disrupting your spirit. The enemy will use your struggles to cause dissension in your marriage and ministry if they are not addressed immediately. This is not the time to start building your First Lady wardrobe or determining your personal ministry. Have the vision for the ministry written out so you can pray and lay hands on it. You must begin to war in the spirit for the success of the vision that God has planted.

Use this time to determine how you will insert yourself into this vision to help it to come to pass. God gives the vision, but uses people to accomplish it within the earthly realm. There are inherent gifts and talents that you possess that will be used to help to bring it to fruition. Some of these giftings are known, some unknown. What does that mean for you? If you can type or file, guess what you'll be doing? If you can sing or dance, guess where you'll be? All gifts are needed in this season in full obedience and submission to the needs and requirements of the ministry.

Being well-versed in the vision will allow you to assist your husband by bringing an added layer of credibility. Intelligently articulating God's calling for your lives and the application of such in your ministry is a form of evangelism. People are not going to want what you're selling unless you can explain to them the reason they should choose your ministry over the one down the street. God will send the people, but you've got to be able to convince them of His benefits concerning your ministry. That's one of the initial reasons He sends the vision: to prove to the people that you and your husband are called according to His purpose.

All about you

It's important to understand that when God called your husband to ministry, He called you too! Let that sink in for a moment. Although ministry is difficult, it is also rewarding, and definitely a life-changing experience. It is easier to do it alone than with an unwilling spouse at your side. Imagine how it would feel to drag around a one hundred fifty-pound sack of potatoes with you everywhere you go. Sound a bit tiring and cumbersome? This is how a husband may feel if his spouse refuses to help in the ministerial work.

Everything becomes more challenging and tedious when you are doing it alone, especially if your spouse is flippant or uncooperative. You must prepare, knowing that as God has joined you two together in marriage (natural), you are also joined together in ministry (spiritual).

Howbeit that was not first which is spiritual, but that which is natural; and afterward that which is spiritual (1 Corinthians 15:46).

Scripture says: A house divided cannot stand. And if a house be divided against itself, that house cannot stand (Mark 3:25). This scripture can also be applied to a marriage. It cannot shoulder the burden of division or two visions.

As God has called your husband, you must follow. Not only follow but support, sustain, and help the vision to come to life. God has planted the vision within your husband for the ministry, and it will only be revealed by the blood, sweat and tears of hard work. Don't let your husband shoulder this responsibility alone. My husband often tells me that I'm the most difficult member of the church! It should not be this way. We should be the most willing, supportive cheerleaders of our husband's ministerial work.

The importance of submission

One sunny day, before the ministry started, as I stood in the doorway of our home watching our dog in the backyard, God spoke to me. He said, "If you don't submit to your husband, you will cause the ministry to fail." As the weight of this revelation began to sink in, I began to feel a series of emotions: shock, belligerence, then fear. *What? Me?* I wondered. *Am I that important in this process that I can shut this whole thing down?*

Like Sarah, I laughed at God, which is one thing that you should not do, because He began to show me specific examples of what He was talking about. Eve, acting on her own authority by eating of the fruit. Sarah, encouraging Abraham to lie with Hagar. Again Sarah, laughing at God. These scenarios depicted wives acting on their own authority and causing shipwrecks. Then God showed me women who I'd met. He showed me pastors' wives who were so far out of their proper position that it had caused their churches to flounder, stifle, and languish, resulting in a failure to thrive and a spiritual standstill.

That message I understood with absolute clarity. There was no way I was going to have all that blood on my hands. It would not be my fault if my husband's church were to crumble. At that moment, I determined that I would fully submit to my husband in ministry. I would allow him to lead, and I would follow.

I felt grateful, as if God had given me a valuable piece of inside information that would help me in the future. I'd already learned the importance of submission in previous studies of scripture but I now had a real-life application. Since I had fully accepted the responsibility to support my husband, I suddenly desired to become the stability that he needed to succeed. I wanted to be a strong beam that would be used to help sustain what he would build under God's anointing, not a person who would tear down and cause destruction. I felt the burden, yet at the same time I began to understand that my role as a pastor's wife was not one of weakness, but of immense power.

What kind of power? I'm referring to the kind of power that if wielded in the wrong manner could dismantle, damage, and destroy God's plans. This served as a colossal wake-up call for me and a tremendously humbling experience. It is one that I have never forgotten, which I believe was God's intent. It serves as a constant reminder as to what is required of me.

What's so hard about it?

Why is it so difficult to be a pastor's wife? The pastor does all the work, one would say. He's the one preaching and ministering; his wife is just sitting there, so what's the big deal? The primary issue of difficulty is the call. God has called your husband; he's had a supernatural experience (most times) where God has summoned him and given him an assignment. He has the burden of the request because of the directional instruction that was received from God.

As for the wife, most often, she has not had that same experience and may not desire to travel down the same path as her husband. Be aware that once the assignment has been issued to your husband, it sets your household in an upheaval. The focus shifts to ministry, and the balance will more than likely remain in ministry from that moment on. This is your new reality, and you'll have to learn to live with it.

Friends and family are forced to deal with you through the paradigm of the ministry. You may often become frustrated as there is increased scrutiny, more demands on your time, more demonic attacks and supernatural occurrences. You may begin to experience additional stress as you deal with variant personalities and their associated problems. There's less time for friends, hobbies and personal endeavors. Furthermore, people will begin to treat you differently once they find out who you are and what you do.

This doesn't even begin to include the changes that God will require of you. As He molds you for this role, you may have to give up certain things at His request. There will be books that you can no longer read, music that you are unable to listen to, and TV shows, and movies censored to you by the Lord. There will also be places that you cannot frequent because the Holy Spirit will convict you to the point of being uncomfortable. Some habits will have to die; even things that you didn't realize were spiritually harmful will have to be jettisoned from your life. Emotions will rage inside of you as God is refining and preparing you. You will begin to realize that you are called to make a sacrifice so that He can get the glory. Old things can't be taken into the new land that you now walk in. Allow yourself to be pruned. Release and relinquish those things in your life to God as He molds you.

There will be times when you'll yearn for someone to help or advise you. You can't "Google" this to find the answer; there's no hotline to call for advice. You pray and ask God, but sometimes you won't get a response. He hears us, but our faith is being tried. As it says in the book of James, patience is having her perfect work in us.

God will abundantly reward you for the sacrifices you make and in the end, you'll be so glad that you did the things requested of you. Often, you cannot see God's hand in motion, but as you progress along His path, you'll be able to look back over your life and see His purpose overlying each specification that was required of you.

There are wolves in sheep's clothing; so, as we PWs are finding our way, one of our responsibilities is to be on the watch for those who desire to smite the shepherd and scatter the sheep. In addition, we must be on alert for those who purposely cause dissension in ministry. There are individuals who instigate church splits and walkouts, people who question the leadership and try to usurp the authority of the pastor. There is difficulty trusting in leadership circles and hesitancy to befriend or advise based on past experiences or hurtful encounters with those who've said, "God has sent me." Lastly, there's jealousy. Plainly, the "crab in a barrel" syndrome, where those in authority do not want to see anyone get ahead or surpass them. They will use any tactic to keep you from moving forward and cause you to doubt God's calling on your life.

The spirit of Jezebel has a cyclical, seasonal mode of attack on ministry (this could be an entire book on its own); you will have to learn to identify and defeat this spirit and be prepared to deal with it again and again. Combine all of this with a feeling of isolation. More than likely, most of your friends are not in ministry, so they will not be able to relate or help you to navigate in these areas. Add in fear, uncertainty, and stress; you now see why some say that it is difficult. It's difficult for those who are in ministry for the right reason: to serve God. Many are just in it for the money and some for power and control.

In all of this, there's a challenge for the PW to find a compassionate ear to listen or even someone to offer advice. Sure, we can always seek God in prayer, however, there are often occasions when we feel the need for human counsel to gain a better perspective. As you look around your circle, you'll often find few, if any, to support you during these times.

Prepare for launch

My husband launched the ministry in 2002. As we started, I was at a loss trying to find my place. We were a new ministry without much support, so we bumbled our way through things the first few years. Looking back, I see now that as I started in my role as the pastor's wife, I failed. I helped my husband administratively by typing, making flyers, greeting the people, smiling, teaching Sunday school, but that's pretty much all that I did.

My husband carried the ministerial burden alone. I was unprepared and felt unequipped to handle the position of the pastor's wife. I began to allow my fears to overtake me. My insecurities of coming to Christianity later in life became my handicap. I physically moved, from the front row of the church to the very last row, and I stayed there for nine years. During that time, I did as little as possible.

Enveloped in fear, I declined and denied all requests that were made of me: to speak, minister, or facilitate events and groups. My husband shouldered the burden of the ministry alone. I am fortunate that this did not impact my marriage. He was accustomed to me dodging responsibilities and dragging my feet. He just continued to pray for me, believing that one day

I would yield to God's calling and assume my proper place.

During those years, our children were born; I used each as a further excuse not to do things in the ministry. I'd say I was too busy being a mom to help out. "The kids need me" was a constant refrain as I sat in the back row and continued to do nothing. Prophetic men and women would come to the church and prophesy that, "they saw me in the front" and told me to "move to the front, woman of God," but I didn't listen. I did not want to listen. Fear turned me into a selfish and self-centered person, so concerned with what others thought of me that I was unable to move forward spiritually or physically.

I didn't want to move forward. I just wanted this scenario to be over and to go back to a church where I could just be a member and not a pastor's wife. Ironically, the church life I'd formerly disliked became very attractive to me. I longed for the days when I could worship, listen to the message and then return home free of responsibilities.

I'm just the pastor's wife

As the PW, what is your role? Most seem to know what the pastor does, but what about his wife? Who defines that role for you? Do you base it on what you've seen in your church life experience? What you've seen in movies or on TV or what your favorite pastor's wife does?

When I became a PW, I started looking around for a role model. I wanted someone I could emulate, someone with attributes and qualities that I could incorporate into my role. I wanted a woman who I could copy to quickly assist me with learning how to be a good pastor's wife. I wanted to be prepared so that when a sticky situation arose, I would be able to say to myself, "What would Lady So-and-So do?" Unfortunately, I came up empty-handed. For those PWs who I could think of, I could find none who I wanted to be like. I wanted to be more real, more savvy, more loving than those I'd experienced. I wanted to just be me.

One day, God told me that I should quit looking and use Him as a role model. Finally, I knew I'd gotten the answer I'd been seeking. I felt relieved that God had given me a real solution, but it was a challenging task to use Him as the archetype. I knew I wouldn't have easy answers by copying someone else, and I'd now have to strenuously strive to measure up to His precedents.

PW, your role is to be defined by your husband. God has placed him as the head of the ministry, and your job is to do whatever the he wants you to do. As his helpmeet, you are to work with him (not as co-pastor; more about that later) as his wife and help cover the needs of the ministry.

I mistakenly believed that my only requirements were to submit to my husband and be his helpmeet. These two qualities are merely the starting foundational points for a PW. You have a responsibility to the women of the church. Whether you like it or not, you are their spiritual mother. It's your choice to determine how you will parent them. If you refuse to accept your role, you become a spiritual parent *in absentia*. This means that you are purposely avoiding responsibility while your children suffer from lack of care.

If you do not assume your proper position, you are neglecting your God-given responsibility to mother the flock that He has assigned to you as the pastor's wife.

You are also a role model to all married couples in your church as an authentication of a Christian wife. Your responsibility is to minister to and speak into the lives of the female members of your church. If they ask you for prayer or counsel, you are the woman of wisdom assigned to that house. You should be able to disseminate biblical wisdom in ways that apply to their tests and trials. The Bible says the elder women are to teach and train the younger women. When we abdicate our role as the PW because of fear or insecurity, we are only presenting half of the spiritual parentage required for balanced ministry. Just as children function best when they're reared in a two-parent household, spiritual children benefit from a two-parent ministry.

In addition, you are your husband's support. You are there to pray for him, counsel and protect him as he goes about his pastoral duties. You are his eyes and ears where he cannot see or hear. Should he ask you to handle a ministerial assignment, preach a sermon or form a book club, you should do it with joy and gladness. Don't complain or delegate, do it yourself. God will anoint you to finish the work. Be happy in the fact that you are helping to take some of the pressure off your husband so that he can effectively run the church.

Until you get comfortable within your proper place in the ministry, what should you do? You support your man. You make sure that he has everything he needs to be the best pastor he can be. From clean underwear to a healthy sex life, it's your job to make sure all bases are covered. Don't shirk responsibility in this area. You must become the most attentive listener to his sermons. Be the best student in his Bible study class. We don't need role models for this; it's common sense and should come naturally. Seems easy, doesn't it? Well, that part is. The problems begin when the members of the church start to arrive.

The coming of the sheep

Increase is exciting. God is beginning to expand the ministry and the people begin to arrive. The pace quickens as things start to get serious. Faith begins to increase as you see God's hand in motion bringing in those who'll require your tutelage. Organization is paramount during this time. The people who God assigns to you will need to see order. They'll need an abundance of love and care from you and your husband as well as a strong spiritual diet rich in scripture. Teaching has never been more important. This is great; it's the honeymoon phase of ministry. All is exciting and new, but in short order, the real work begins.

These lovely people each bring their own mixed bag of problems, grievances, and desires. It will be up to you and your husband to love the "hell" out of them. They will make you earn your stripes as you learn to handle their concerns, complaints and criticisms. You'll minister them through their pain. You both will aid them in being set free and delivered from oppression all through the grace administered to you by the Holy Spirit.

After most services, there will be those with problems or needs that will have to be addressed immediately. Personality clashes, fights, and jealousy tend to run rampant through congregations. Often, the pastor is left to resolve these burdens alone. His response (or lack of) may cause congregants to become bitter and leave the ministry if not properly handled.

This is a thankless part of the work that you do because many want you to labor with them in counseling, prayer, healing, and deliverance. Many will leave once they are free or receive the thing that caused them to initially seek God, just as the lepers Jesus healed in Luke 17. Ten were cleansed, yet nine ran off once they got what they needed.

There is a continual stream of requests and inquiries from congregants that must be effectively handled: prayer, counseling, financial, etc. If not properly addressed, they may flow into your personal lives and push familial issues to the side. At times, your family and friends will voice concerns that you're spending too much time on church issues and responsibilities. They may even guilt-trip you into procuring a more balanced life.

Everything that you have ever learned will be put to the test during this phase. These groups of people who are assigned to your ministry and under your guidance will need to be transformed into warriors for Christ. You must teach them to war, fight, overtake, and overcome the hand of the enemy. They'll need to learn to pray, worship, study, seek God, and to line their lives up with scripture.

This particular aspect of ministry requires a lot of work. You'll need to stand on 1 Corinthians 13 because love is the most important component. You love God, and this gives you the strength and fortitude to handle the people, personalities, and problems that come to your ministry. Love covers a multitude of sins. My husband says, "The church is a hospital. If their lives were perfect and they didn't have insurmountable problems they wouldn't seek after Jesus." Prepare to jump in the trenches; God engineered you for this specific task.

Cavalcade of the inconceivable

We must never shun or turn anyone away in the church. Regardless of their appearance, lack of hygiene, or any physical condition, all should be welcome in God's house. He is the one doing the work; we are merely tools used for His service. My husband says, "Once people get around the fire, they will start to get warm." Let God clean them up; you concentrate on loving, teaching, and providing a nurturing place for them.

Jesus says, "Come unto me, all ye that labour and are heavy laden, and I will give you rest" (Matthew 11:28). It is true some will be tired and overburdened, but you will also have drug addicts, pedophiles, pathological liars, thieves, murderers, terminally ill, victims of abuse, etc. Those who come to your ministry should get the best you have to offer because Jesus said, "Inasmuch as ye have done it unto one of the least of these my brethren, ye have done it unto me" (Matthew 25:40).

Many years ago, I was visiting a church, and two teenaged girls walked in mid-service. They were wearing mini-skirts and revealing necklines, and they looked as if they'd just come from a nightclub. They caused a bit of a stir as they found their seats. As they sat and began to listen to the sermon, the pastor's wife came and whispered in their ears. They both immediately stood to their feet and walked out of the church and did not return.

I've often wondered what was said to those two girls. How, regardless of their appearance, something made them hunger for God on that particular day. They might have sought out that ministry, desiring an outpouring of love or something they desperately needed. How was it that they were made to feel unwelcome in God's house? Was that PW so insecure? Was she just having a bad day? Did she possess so much of a religious spirit that she couldn't plainly see two hurting souls? Didn't she realize that God would hold her accountable for her actions? My brethren, be not many masters, knowing that we shall receive the greater condemnation (James 3:1).

There's nothing more transformative than an encounter with the living God. You must ensure that your ministry is a house of healing, love, and restoration. As Jesus said, "They that are whole have no need of the physician, but they that are sick" (Mark 2:17). There are many stories in Scripture of leaders having to build downtrodden miscreants into mighty warriors of the Most High. Always attempt to help those who the Lord brings across your path to the best of your ability.

The books

One day, one of the members of our church shared with me a book on being a pastor's wife. She was a former pastor's wife and thought it would be helpful for me because it had been useful for her. She'd witnessed my struggle and noticed how I continually sat in the back. This woman had also been the recipient of one of my many refusals to help in ministry. I accepted the book and read it. My usual habit is that one book leads me to another, then another. However, after reading several books on the subject of being a pastor's wife, I was now thoroughly confused.

First, I became depressed. I read one book authored by a PW who seemed like a Christian version of Martha Stewart. She would color code everything, use index filing, and had obsessive organizational skills so precise that I could not actually believe the words this woman had written. It made me feel like a failure as I thought of my scrap note filled purse and disorganized files. I thought I could never, ever be like that woman.

Next, I read books that were tomes of plaintive common sense advice coupled with witty anecdotes that failed to inspire any hope in me. Finally, after reading the last book, I realized I had not found the book that I desperately needed to read. I couldn't find anyone who was writing about the things that were troubling me and substantially affecting my church life and role as the PW. Why, I thought to myself; is there no book written in regards to real truths? Is it because I'm from an African American church and our problem set is so vastly unique? Or is it just not polite to air our dirty laundry? Ultimately, I ended up donating all the books about pastor's wives to a book swap. They didn't help me at all.

I now realize that the black church experience is not unique. The woes felt by most pastors' wives are universally shared experiences. The problem is that it is not polite or scriptural (which is far more important) to air our grievances. Even today, when I encounter other PWs, we tend to skirt around issues, attempt to make small talk and play nice, not touching the topics that weigh heavily on our shoulders and in our spirits.

I began to think; *Maybe I should write a book about PWs. I should write about the information that I've been seeking and answer the questions that I haven't been able to get a reply to. Perhaps I should broach those topics and share my experiences.* But, I thought, *Am I being directed by the flesh or Spirit?* To date, I have not received an answer.

I started this work nine years ago. During that time, the book you are now holding began as my personal, private rant. I used this writing as a safe place to vent and sort through some of the things that I was experiencing. I constantly felt as if I didn't have anyone to talk to. I felt completely misunderstood.

In the past three years, I've found myself sharing the information written here with new PWs. They've told me it was helpful, and I began to look at these writings in a new way. I started to keep a copy of them in my purse and would often hand it to a new PW I'd met after I'd find myself repeating verbatim some of the sections I'd written privately.

I believe now is the time to share especially when I see PWs hurting and confused as I was so many years ago. Reluctantly, I started to format these writings into a book because I am now in a position to help others. God would not be pleased if I stood by and watched other PWs suffer when I can share with those walking on the same path I'd previously been on.

My original intention was not to write a book, but to get some help. At this point in my life, I am in a place of healing. Throughout this journey, God has taught me some things, people have taught me some things, and experience has taught me some things. I am now ready to share in the hope that I may repay by helping those who may be experiencing similar situations.

Your gifts

God has given you specific areas of gifting in your life. They are inherent abilities that allow you to excel in certain areas where others may struggle. You were born with them. Is this important in ministry? Absolutely. It is vital that you define and understand your areas of expertise to help your husband within the ministry. They are needed in each ministerial phase: the conception, gestation, birth, and matriculation of the church.

Your gifts correspond (not compete) with the gifts in your husband. They fit together like puzzle pieces. My husband is strong in leadership and architecture; I am strong in administration and infrastructure. If you do not know where your gifts lie, I would suggest taking one of those "Spiritual Gift Assessment" quizzes that you can readily find online. There are many different versions, and the results will give you a general indication of the areas where your gifts reside. If this is not an option, look at the type of work that you do; often, we are in positions where we unknowingly utilize our gifts each day. Or look at the things you enjoy doing; such as hobbies and favorite pastimes may often be rooted in areas of gifting.

Perhaps you and your spouse share the same gifting, as my husband and I share the teaching gift. My abilities correspond and compliment his. They never overrule or engulf. You must be willing to submit your areas of gifting to help with the success of the ministry. This was purposed by the Lord. He specifically equipped you with certain skills that need to be used for His Glory in ministry. Understand that no gift is too small or too inconsequential to God. It is far more important that you are yielded to His will and willing to do whatever is necessary regardless of any fear or insecurities you may feel.

A man's gift makes room for him, and bringeth him before great men (Proverbs 18:16). Some of your areas of gifting are easily identifiable. You can easily note the application of them within your church. Others are more difficult to pinpoint. Do not despair; there will come a time when you'll know exactly how your skillset corresponds directly with your assignment. Don't be surprised; there are often hidden areas of gifting that we aren't even aware of until we start working in ministry. Things that you didn't even know that you could do may pop up seemingly out of nowhere – know that God has purposed this.

Take a good, hard look at yourself

This isn't the time for smoke and mirrors or rose-colored glasses. You will need to examine your effectiveness in ministry as a PW and make changes, if necessary. As we start on this journey, we often make many mistakes; lessons are learned, and hopefully, improvements are made. It is necessary to take stock of who you are right now, what you are doing right now, and planning on doing in the future concerning your role as a PW.

Look around. Are you impactful in the church or just being a bump on a log? A seat holder? A sanctified mannequin sitting in the first row? If you're not doing anything, you are not helping your husband, and it could be negatively impacting your ministry. What's the best way to deal with this situation?

Ask your husband, "Honey, I'd like to be more active in the church. Where do you need my help?" Do whatever he asks of you. Try to do it without questioning and to the best of your ability. Get some books if the topics are unfamiliar to you and become an expert in whatever area you are needed.

Conversely, are you doing too much? Are you in church each day and night, constantly in conferences, counseling, and convocations with little time for your husband to assess his needs? Talk to him; ask if he feels that you are not devoting enough time to assist with his ministerial needs.

As a PW, you do not measure yourself against some archetype. You measure against what your husband needs you to do in the ministry. Forget what the congregants say; your husband is the leader who God has placed in that church. His voice is the one that you must abide by. People come and go; we'll never garner the pleasure of man's favorable opinion. Naysayers are in abundance, particularly in the church, where most are quick to vocalize our shortcomings and deficiencies. Moses got in trouble when he acted out of frustration because of what the people were saying instead of following the instructions of God. This is all the more reason for us to be in alignment with our husbands as they lead God's people.

We cannot outsource our responsibilities as a PW. As long as your husband is the pastor, he is going to need his wife to assist him. Nobody can do what you do for him, and no one else should do what you do for him. You must accept that as your new reality and make room for it in your life. Schedule it as an annual event: Once a year, re-evaluate your position to make sure you are exactly where your husband needs you to be.

The shifting

The life that I knew was about to change. 2009 was the year our world would turn upside down, and our lives would shift forever. We'd just had our third child in 2008. When she was ten months old, my mother-in-law suddenly passed away. We'd made her a grandmother, and she never had a chance to fully enjoy the little girls she'd always wanted.

In quick succession, we lost more family members: my husband's grandfather and his uncle. We even lost our beloved dog that we'd had for ten years prior to our children being born. Reeling with grief, my husband officiated his mother's funeral. Later that year, he began to experience an unrelated health issue and he became extremely ill. As he spent time in the hospital, his presence in our church services decreased. The leaders he had trained and depended on began to weaken under the strain of his absence. As he asked them to step up and help more during this time of need, they countered that he should shut the church down and abandon all that he was doing for the Lord.

The entire time my husband was hurting, grieving, and in the midst of his own health crisis, church members continued to selfishly demand counseling and attention concerning their personal problems.

It was during this time that I began to notice that these sheep would gladly kill their shepherd. All my husband had done for them personally did not matter during his period of crisis. They would suck him dry and move on. I could no longer sit idle in that back row. I began to feel immense anger toward the people and the position they were putting my family and husband through. I didn't know at the time that I should've prayed and sought the Lord. Instead, I got up and moved to the front of the church to start helping my husband in ministry.

CHAPTER

TWO

Suffer in silence?

Many years have passed since I've written the words in the beginning of this book. I have more experience, wisdom, and insight into the role of the PW. I have abandoned my search for a mentor, role model, or best friend. The role of the PW seems to require that I walk without a confidant; instead, I have Jesus as my BFF. I've met women through ministry; even though I've attempted to get close to them, many of those relationships have not blossomed into friendships that I feel are needed at this stage of my life. The types of ministry friendships that I have are not the same types of worldly friendships I had before I became a PW. I no longer seek to pattern my behavior as other PWs may do. Instead, I rely on God. Perhaps this is what I was supposed to do all along.

The realities of serving the Lord have made me more stoic. Yes, there are times I suffer in silence. There are times when burdens weigh heavily on my shoulders and in my spirit. I have attempted to discuss my concerns with my husband, and his suggestion is to have me speak with one of his pastor friends who is female. I bristle at this each time, telling him that his friends are not what I need at a time like this; I need my own counsel.

So, the real issues are: Are you unable to make friends because of the position you are in? Does your role as a PW make you feel that you must suffer alone? Are you afraid to confide in the female members of your church because they may betray your confidence or lose respect for you? Are you unable to get answers from worldly friends because they aren't saved or "don't know the ways of the church"? Again, many questions but no answers.

I would say, in retrospect, that I've learned to trust Jesus. I don't say that in a patronizing manner but in absolute truthfulness. There are certain answers that you can only get from Him. When there is no answer, you must bravely soldier on.

Yes, it's a lonely road

Friends may be few and confidants even fewer. This may be a lonely time in your life, but not in the way you may think. You have a full calendar, more than enough to do, lots of activities, and lots of people surrounding you but it's lonely. Many PWs speak of the loneliness they feel, isolation in a room full of many. They may be unable to trust others because of the position they are in with their husband in the ministry.

People have a tendency to sometimes think PWs are unapproachable and will not ask them on lunch dates. You may not get invited to outings because the person asking may feel they'll have to act "holy" the entire time and can't be themselves. You can't really pal around with members of the church because they may feel the PW is a tattle teller who will reveal secrets or indiscretions to her husband the pastor. So, often, you are not included.

Making friends with other PWs can be difficult. I have found it to be a daunting task. There are some who I have loved and some I didn't like so much. There are some who have spoken words of wisdom to me and others who have ignored me. There are some women who I've met and connected with strongly (I thought), only to be rebuffed when I tried to arrange lunch dates or get close to them. I can't explain these complicated dynamics between PWs, but it's ridiculous. The only other thing I've experienced similarly is the light-skinned/dark-skinned rivalry that goes on between some African-American women.

Currently, I do not have many PW friends. I don't even try

anymore. This is the path that I have chosen to walk in this phase of my life. Perhaps, it may change in five years. I have learned that this is not about how I may feel or what I may need, but more in regard to the work that God wants to be done. It's not about being bitter; it's just that I am on assignment.

He's the pastor, so what am I?

Co-pastor? Evangelist? Prophetess? Who am I? Just because your husband is now called pastor, don't feel the need to assume a competing title. Don't feel that you should change or subvert your identity to equate with his elevation. If you previously functioned as an evangelist or prophetess, then by all means, you must continue. If you were previously "sister", then just be the pastor's wife.

 I've seen far too many wives jump into titles because their husband does. He's the pastor, so now you must be co-pastor? *Correct?* Absolutely not, unless God has called you to that office, do not change your title. Your husband is the apostle, so now you're a prophetess? Beware! If God has not appointed you to walk in that office, then don't do it.

Why are women afraid to just be called the pastor's wife? My personal opinion? It's not a glorious or highly lauded role. It's often the PW who must deal with the mundane tasks, so most people perceive her to be meek, humble, quiet, and boring. If you refer to yourself as "First Lady", which is her glamorous counterpart, you are suddenly esteemed, elegant, and regal. I believe that if the PW feels the need to assume another title (e.g., prophetess, evangelist) without God's involvement, this allows her to craft her own ministerial profile.

This, my friends, is a display of self-importance and arrogance when the pastor's wife feels the need to overstate her gifts and calling, so that people will openly acknowledge her presence, stature, and contribution. As I have stated previously: *What is wrong with just being the pastor's wife?* Before ministry, you were his wife, and you were fine with that. So why does the foray into ministry make wives so insecure in their calling and ability that they become self-conscious attention seekers? As my husband says, "You make the title; the title does not make you." Let God change your title through His elevations, not one born from a position of personal pride. All you need to do is start by being the best PW that you can conceivably be. How do we do that? By instituting a level of pastoral care that no one on earth can do better than you.

Co-pastor: two heads are better than one?

When couples begin their ministry, they may sometimes share the leadership role. The husband is the pastor, and his wife will be co-pastor. I find this role interesting in that the prefix "co-" denotes joint or mutual. So, if you are called co-pastor, then your ministry has dual leadership. Your husband will be the head of the ministry and you are the joint head.

When Adam began his work for God, he was charged with dressing and keeping of the garden. God determined that Adam needed a helpmeet. Thus, we see the creation of Eve as his support. The moment Eve operated outside of her role, she caused Adam to make a tremendous mistake, resulting in the fall of man.

Your ministry does not require two heads. God places one person in authority of His church, and everybody else is the help. As God came walking through the garden after they had partaken of the fruit, He called out to Adam. And the Lord God called unto Adam, and said unto him, Where art thou? (Genesis 3:9). He was not looking for Eve. He was looking for the person who He placed in authority.

The Bible says that God does not change. For I am the Lord, I change not… (Malachi 3:6). He is the same today and forever.

If your husband is the pastor, why can't his wife simply be his wife? Your designation as co-pastor creates confusion for the members. Who should they see, you or your husband? Will the congregation see this as some type of competition going on between you two? Are you saying it is okay for you to submit to your husband in marriage, but in ministry you are equal? What does God say concerning that?

I believe that as a pastor's wife you can be a minister, pastor, associate pastor, or whatever role God has called you to. However, in leadership, you are not equivalent to your husband, the pastor. As my husband says, "Anything that has more than one head is considered a freak of nature." I feel that pastors' wives will jump into the co-pastor role because it gives validity to their leadership role in the ministry, enabling them to demand respect when, in fact, it should be earned. As I've previously stated, PWs are often looked down upon. I believe that some PWs assume a title because they feel it helps alleviate their feelings of insecurity of "just being the pastor's wife".

Cover: a lesson from Ham

My husband often jokes that if he would ask me to lie for him, I would not. That if there was even a remote possibility of him going to jail and I was the key witness, I would tell the truth before perjuring myself in a bid to see him go free. I smile when he says it during his sermons, because it's true. I do not struggle between telling the truth concerning matters versus covering or exposing my husband. For me, the truth is always right.

I have had the unfortunate experience of being around several PWs who were more than willing to slander their husband's name and reputation. This was because of sinful action(s) that were committed. One PW aired all of her husband's personal indiscretions, discrediting him, avenging herself and making all his peers feel that he was a fraud. Right? Wrong! What had transpired was that one of God's servants was exposed by someone so close to him that she had an unfair advantage (hint: Samson and Delilah). This woman had the ability to reveal intimate details that hastened the character assassination of one of God's anointed. Also, she was hurting. We all know hurting people often hurt others.

Be confident in the fact that God will handle those battles. If there is sin present, you can best believe that He is equipped to deal with that situation much better than you can. God is able to work the situation out and restore the individuals involved. You will only wreck things. At the end of your destructive spree, you will be hurting as well as being in the midst of a path of devastation you have created. We must take care, PWs.

When you become aware that your husband has sinned against God, you must first follow the words of Jesus. "Thou hypocrite, first cast out the beam out of thine own eye; and then shalt thou see clearly to cast out the mote out of thy brother's eye" (Matthew 7:5). Pray. Pray for him. Pray for God to help him through this situation.

One day, God told me He wanted me to cover my husband. He led me to Genesis 10 which makes reference to the sons of Noah; specifically Ham, who finds his father drunk and naked in the tent. First, why is Ham spying on his dad? More importantly, when Ham finds the man of God drunk and disorderly, he proceeds to blab to his brothers concerning their father's inebriated state. His two brothers, Shem and Japheth, then go directly to their father's tent, walking in backwards (so they don't see him in the midst of his sin), and cover him with a blanket. This, God says, is what I am to do. He then instructs me if I see or hear something that I must cover my husband. Cover him in prayer, cover him in our life partnership, and cover him with love.

In this age, it is a popular sport to discredit leaders and their ministries. Too many times, we are seeing pastors jailed or persecuted for criminal offenses. The enemy is having a field day in defrauding and attempting to destroy the leadership of the modern church. As Christians, we should not condone sin or lawlessness. Simultaneously, we should not engage in gossip or character assassination of ministerial leaders. Our first response should be to cover them with prayer. God is the Judge. He will handle it, as I have said before; He has the ability to render and execute judgment more effectively than anything we can aspire to do.

People watch you

It's a common joke in ministry that if you want to learn about a pastor, all you have to do is look at his wife. Unfortunately, in my experience, I have found this to be very true. I've been in services where the pastor is in the pulpit preaching fervently, gesticulating wildly, basking in the glow of the Holy Spirit, and his wife is on the front row frowning. I've seen PWs texting while their husbands were preaching. While others talked throughout their sermons. Some looked wounded and hurt during the service, appearing distracted or not paying attention. In some cases, the PW would just get up and leave.

It is important to know that your behavior is noted and noticed by most. As PWs, we must be careful of what we present to the public eye. Things that we say or do can reflect badly on our husbands and may unintentionally cause people to leave the ministry.

A lesson I learned the hard way is you should not joke or play around with the members of the church as a PW. Comments that you consider humorous may wound people or cause deep offense. While you may apologize, those words can never be retracted. When your husband is ministering, you should be in rapt attention of what he is saying. If you have had any prior marital arguments or conflicts, they have no place in the church during services. This type of selfish behavior makes your husband look bad while making you look like a mean, controlling Jezebel. It can even affect your husband's ability to minister if he sees you scowling.

How would you feel if you were ministering in the pulpit and saw that type of facial expression on your spouse? So, please, watch your expressions, postures, and dispositions while your husband is ministering; the people, and God, are watching you.

Have you eaten?

One of the biggest mistakes I have made is the expectation that I go to church as a PW to be fed. Each Sunday, I would attentively listen to my husband preach, all the while seeking nourishment and revelation from his God-inspired words. I would struggle to relate the themes to my personal life, often asking God, "How does this apply to me?" Even while typing his sermon notes for him at home before church services, I would try to read between the lines, attempting to discern why God was directing him to minister in such ways and wrestling with a personal application of the teachings.

Often, I'd feel unsatisfied, as if I hadn't enough to eat. I'd feel as though I was still spiritually hungry. I needed more to make it through my own personal tests and trials. I knew my husband preached "a good word", yet it wasn't a word for me. Why? Where was my much-needed instructional knowledge and teaching?

As with all things that seem to happen to me, over time, the Holy Spirit began to show me what was happening. God began to reveal that I was going to church in the wrong position. My time of being someone who could sit and feast on the word was over. My posture was incorrect. I held the belief I was coming to receive, but the Holy Spirit told me that I must come to *give*. The reason you are having a hard time applying that word to your life is because it isn't for you. No longer do you attend service as a lay member; you must listen to the sermons with a different ear.

Instead of thinking *How does this apply to me?* It should now be...*How can I assist my husband in the application of these teachings?* How can these ministrations be effectively disseminated for maximum impact? The Bible says that immediately after the word has been sown, the enemy shows up. ...Satan cometh immediately, and taketh away the word that was sown in their hearts (Mark 4:15). So now, as a PW, my role is to become a defensive line for the word that God ministers in the house. No longer am I able to soak in the words, but I must posture to defend them to those who have missed or had the words stolen from them by the enemy before they reach home.

God showed me that He would make sure I was fed, even in my wilderness experience as a PW. As He sent ravens to feed Elijah, I too would be nourished. I had to have faith in Him. Surely, as I have obeyed, God has made good on His promise.

As a PW, you are no longer just a church member, even if you are not holding an active position in the ministry. The fact that you're the pastor's wife separates you from every other person in that building. In each area that your husband is called to minister, you are called to support. For his call, you are the compliment. As he ministers, you are his helpmeet and protection. God sent the Holy Spirit to teach you in all things, so put your notebook away and pull out your strategy book.

Offended?

There will be times when you may offend people in your church either knowingly or unknowingly. Let's discuss this. When you deliberately offend, shame on you. Some examples would be criticizing, being overly harsh, ignoring people, and not showing love to people in your ministry. We should not be doing that as PWs. We should instead try to uplift and encourage the membership, not tear them down; they get enough of that out in the world.

When you unknowingly offend someone, it is best handled by you apologizing directly to that person straightaway. This serves as a reminder to yourself to never repeat such an insulting action. You do not want to be the reason a person leaves a church. Try and resolve any issues that stem from your actions.

When the shoe is on the other foot, and one of the members offends you, what do you do? My advice is to turn the other cheek. I have had many people say things to me over the years that may be considered belligerent, mean, or outright rude. I've had people comment on my appearance, marriage, children, etc. As I have previously mentioned, it is important that we as PWs conduct ourselves as leaders. For those who lash out at us in an offensive manner, first, you must realize that they are hurting and often do not know how to properly express or deal with their pain. Secondly, you must recognize that this is rooted in a spiritual attack against you.

Look at the demon behind this attack and not the person who is being used to confront you. Finally, ask yourself: "What Would Jesus Do"? If we yield to the flesh to resolve this manner, it will most likely not glorify Jesus. More realistically, it could get you into trouble with the pastor.

Warning: Sheep may attack

One of the things I learned very quickly in ministry was to prepare for attacks. I assumed falsely that most attacks would be demonic in nature as I began my studies in spiritual warfare and learning how to bind up demons. The demons did attack, but I was more surprised by the ferocity of an attack that came from the sheep. There were times when members of the church would try to demean, belittle or put me down as the pastor's wife. Over the years, I have developed a tough skin, and those things no longer beset me. I now see them as the enemy's attempt to get me off focus. These days, I focus on the person making those remarks, knowing that the devil is using them, and I must keep an eye on them to determine their intent.

Some church members have openly tried to discredit me by

calling my husband crying, complaining that I have said words they consider to be hurtful or malicious. They have even insinuated that I was mean or mean-spirited, and my husband has had to moderate the situation in order to restore harmony. The end result is that I receive a stern talking-to. What I've learned from these experiences is to keep my husband involved in all potentially problematic situations as much as possible. When members are upset at what I have done, I apologize and try to correct the situation. At the same time alerting my husband to the problem that I may have created and taking responsibility for my actions.

I've begun to employ the use of discernment, and the study of body language and nonverbal cues. If you are not prophetic, I would highly recommend visiting your local library and getting some books on these topics as they may come in handy. Often, you will be able to determine a person's intent before the attack is launched. If you miss cues, and a member is intent on lashing out at you, defer to your husband. After all, he is the one God has placed in authority of the church, so let him handle and resolve the situation. Over the years, I've learned that members respond more willingly to my husband, even when he and I are saying the same thing. They tend to readily acknowledge the pastor since God has appointed him as the angel of that house.

Church at home/Home at church

In political circles, there are often discussions regarding the separation of church and state. In the Christian community, especially in the pastor's home, that separation becomes pretty thin. At times, your ministry is like a member of your family. When my husband first started our church, he went through a gestational period then birthed out this thing that required lots of care and constant attention. We spent hours talking strategy, making provisions, preparing, praying, launching, and working to bring the vision that God had given my husband into the earthly realm. Personal ministry and our church are constant streams of discussion in our lives; it's a part of who we are, and for us, there really is no separation.

Pillow talk often concerns ministry. Dinner talk often involves ministry. Vacations and date nights involve ministry, even when we attempt to discuss other topics. If you love something, you will find yourself continually thinking of that thing. That is how we both feel about God's house. We take our roles seriously and will often bounce things off each other to make sure we are doing the correct things for the church. It is stressful, especially if you have kids; they demand attention too. They are not as understanding of the lengthy phone calls, counseling sessions, strategy meetings and other activities that are needed. You will find that you may have to institute downtime to keep a balanced household.

I've often encountered people who tell me they grew up as preacher's kids or "PKs" as they are fondly known. They tell stories of how, as children, they were constantly in church and had little time to do other things. As they grew older, they began to resent the church, and when they had the first opportunity, they ran as quickly as they could away from church with the intention of never returning. These stories sadden me immensely. As I look at my children, I cannot imagine doing something to them to make them no longer love Jesus or want to serve Him. I tell people that in my pursuit of serving God through ministry, if I turn my kids away from Him, I have failed, and I have defrauded the work of the Lord.

At times, it's difficult to maintain a balance between church and home: ballet lessons versus speaking engagements; play dates versus women's events; school night homework versus weeknight service. Sometimes you win, sometimes you lose. The kids need may need a break; so sometimes my husband goes to ministry events alone. You have to find the balance that works for you and your family.

As a PW, you will find yourself as the one responsible for balancing church, family, and home dynamics within your household. In essence, you literally become the embodiment of a Proverbs 31 woman. You are put directly in the middle. You must learn to navigate these areas and keep order. Your husband, the pastor, will have ministry events that will consume his time; he needs to be taken care of. Make sure he gets proper care to the best of your ability. Often, mighty men of God begin to suffer health ailments as they travel and minister, exhausting their bodies, eating too much fast food while maintaining rigorous schedules.

The children have needs too, so it is up to you as the "air traffic controller" of your household to ensure that everything stays in order. This is no easy task as you may have ministry events and ministerial duties to perform as well. It will feel as if there is no one to take care of you! Regardless, you are required to keep those in your household fed and clothed, and ensure their needs are attended to. Many times, I've had to duck into my prayer closet to seek God's strength to make it through situations like these.

No, it doesn't feel good. No, it doesn't get any easier the more it happens. But by His grace, everything invariably works out somehow in the end, and you make it through in Jesus' name.

When your husband wants to be a superstar preacher

As I write this, I walk in these shoes in my own life. Of all the
seasons in ministry, I find this to be the most difficult one. Let's
say that your husband, the pastor, has been told that he is
supposed to go to the nations to have a national, even global
platform. The prophets tell him that God has called him to
travel the world, sit with politicians, celebrities, people in high
places, and minister to them. That he will connect with
powerful men and women of God and do great things for the
Kingdom.

Does that sound like a great word? One that you'd shout on if
it were given to you? A cause to celebrate? I'm sure most of us
would say: Yes! We love to hear of the saints of God doing
powerful and mighty things for the Kingdom. It's exciting; it
affirms our faith. It's a demonstration of God's power.

All of this is true, but what happens when it comes to your
household? Your husband is that pastor. The speaking
engagements are numerous. So many, in fact, that you can no
longer keep track of them. They interfere with birthdays,
vacations and family events. His time away from home
increases as he begins to fellowship and strategize with mighty
men and women of God. Hours and hours of phone calls,

involvement in events, roundtables, conference calls, luncheons, etc. They flood his life as you stand there watching, not sure what to do. You know your position is to be by your husband's side. Yet, at the same time, you are not able to be present in some of these arenas.

You try your very best as a PW to travel, support, and to assist at times when you're needed. In short season, you find it's not enough. Where the presence of your husband's personal ministry virtually becomes a physical manifestation in the midst of your relationship, both inside and out of the church. Picture this: you're lying in bed at night. It's you, your husband, and his personal ministry, laying there right between you two. It's almost as if it is a physical presence intruding into your everyday lives.

This is tough and can get a bit nasty. In pursuit of his own personal ministry, this season of growth and expansion means the entire family must pay the price. You become displaced, the kids are displaced, and even the dog is displaced as your husband "makes his bones" and "works the chitlin' circuit", preaching, *preaching*, **preaching**, and PREACHING! How does it make you feel? You love your husband. This is what he's been wanting and has worked so hard for, and you're so happy for him. The sacrifices, the blood, sweat, and tears sown into the ministry are beginning to bear fruit, but your personal life is a wreck! It takes everything you have plus furtive trips to the prayer closet to make it through each week.

You start to dread Saturdays and Sundays because there are so many things packed into those two days that you work harder than at your full-time job. Everything is rushed, dinner comes from the "drive-thrus", laundry and dishes pile up, and you can barely keep up. What do you do? Pray. Yes, of course, we're PWs; we're always praying. Your life is chaotic.

How do you handle this? This will make or break you as a PW. You thought you had some tough challenges in the past? Not quite, love; this is a wrecking ball in motion. There are no easy answers during this time of refinement for you as a PW. God is removing the dross from you in this season as your husband's ministry begins to grow and prosper.

Remember that you are the vital link. Know that you must have full confidence in your position and calling in God's Kingdom so that you do not act out of order. As God once told me, if I was out of position, I could cause the ministry to fail; the same is true in the season of expansion.

It's almost as if there's a physical manifestation of the enemy. He speaks often and in subtle ways that cause you to think that his thoughts are your own. Attacks are direct and physical; you now understand why the enemy attempts to cause destruction through the wife. He tempted Eve; he tempted the wives of Lot and Job, and he tempted Sarah. So why not you?

This may be a dangerous time for you. Watch your steps; watch your words in this season. This is a good time to embody the Scriptures: And that ye study to be quiet...(1 Thessalonians 4:11). ...Satan hath desired to have you, that he may sift you as wheat (Luke 22:31). As referred to earlier, Delilah knew exactly what to do to detract and derail God's purpose for Samson. You are in possession of the same knowledge. The fruit of the Spirit must be abundant in your life right now. You will be called to exemplify each one many times.

Remember, although experience can be an excellent instructor it is a difficult teacher. There have been times when the Holy Spirit has come in at the last instance and prevented terrible things from happening by showing me the enemy's hand. I have been so angry with myself for being deceived, but God has shown me that the enemy is so subtle; it is the strong suit he's used to destroy many. By the work of Jesus Christ on the cross, the enemy is defeated. God will warn before destruction, which is why we must be vigilant to hear His voice during this time.

No matter what is going on in your life, never lose communication with God. Don't shut out His voice or pull away from Him. He will be a very present help in time of need, even if you don't realize you need Him to rescue you.

CHAPTER

THREE

That's what friends are for

As your husband climbs the ladder to this national platform, many people will begin to come into his life. Developing friendships in ministry is difficult. When you're aiming at reaching elevated levels of ministry, it is good to have friends in high places. They can help to open doors, procure opportunities, share wisdom, and it looks great. Popularity helps to fill seats.

As his new friends come and go, you are privy to witnessing the underbelly of ministry. Cliques are very much a part of things that happen behind the pulpit. You'll find yourself in the offices and back rooms, hearing gossip and backbiting. There's a teardown and restoration of those working in the pulpits. It feels as if you don't belong in this place. Once you begin to fellowship with those who you've admired from afar, you begin to see their human shortfalls. You start to realize that what you truly admire is the anointing on their lives and not their personalities. At the end of the day, they are men and women as we all are.

Some of these relationships are necessary. Although your discernment may flag around some of these people, you have to learn to temper yourself lest you cause relationships to fail. Believe me, you do have that power. If there's one funky acting pastor's wife in the bunch, it spoils the whole lot. What am I saying? When you discern characteristics in a man or woman in a leadership position, who is attempting to draw close to your husband, your first intent is to sound the alarm. If that warning is not acknowledged by your spouse, you will tend to be more forceful concerning your opinions regarding that leader.

My husband has accused me of being rude toward leaders who he was trying to get close to. Why? Well, my mama bear instinct kicked in! I could no longer stand massive egos in thinly cloaked spirituality, parading around like peacocks. I have such a problem with tomfoolery in God's house that it incites attributes in me that I thought I was delivered from long ago.

Sometimes, my husband tells me that so-and-so preacher is no longer his friend on Facebook. I will often say, "Good, something wasn't right about him anyway." Is this wrong? Yes.

PWs must control themselves. If you see attributes that you don't like; what should you do? Pray. Acting out does not solve anything. It embarrasses your spouse and definitely will not help him to make friends in high places. If you are finding this difficult to deal with, then you should probably stay out of the back rooms with the leadership.

I've got to get away!

Vacation! Yes, make sure that you are doing this. It is important that your husband, the pastor, take a break from time to time. Believe it or not, it's important for the ministry as well. Part of the pastor's assignment is to construct a team so that the vision will manifest within the ministry apart from who the lead pastor may be. Time away gives the senior pastor a much-needed break and contributes to raising up future leaders by giving them opportunities to teach and minister in the absence of the pastor.

Plan a yearly vacation for you and your spouse, make time to relax and unwind. It's good for your health, marriage, and ministry. Have fun, and relieve some of the stress. My husband believes in taking two annual vacations; One is the family getaway, and the second is without the kids so we can spend time sowing back into our marriage. Physically, it is essential to get away. This helps to give you a bit of overview concerning things occurring in your life and your ministry.

Once I heard a pastor say, "Take a vacation and leave your Bible at home!" I thought this was heresy until I began to experience the pressures of ministry. I learned how some time away from everyone and everything can actually increase your relationship with God by allowing you time to balance and refocus. His word is stored in your heart, and you won't believe how clearly you'll hear His voice sitting under palm trees near warm ocean breezes that will restore and replenish.

I want out!

It is normal to want to quit. In fact, at least once a week, I desire to resign my position. I get fed up and frustrated with the machinations of the contemporary Christian church and yearn for a less complicated manner of serving the Lord. "God," I cry, "why is it so difficult just to serve You? I love you, but why do your people give me such a hard time?"

Do not despair! If it were so easy, everyone would be doing it! Know that God will not bring anything to you that He has not already equipped you to handle. In times of frustration, we must dig deep, pray and trust God. He is able. Take one day at a time; solve each problem as it arises and continue to operate in faith. Most importantly, realize that you are not alone. As you are flummoxed and perplexed, so are many who operate in the faith; work in the ministry and serve the Kingdom. We don't quit; we can't quit.

As much as you don't want to admit it, people are watching you, gauging your reactions, and looking for your opinions. As we continually attempt to teach church members to "look to Jesus", they are often looking to their leaders for their actions and reactions. My husband often says: "Sometimes, you are the only Jesus that people will see." You may be the nearest representative of Christ that some individuals will ever interact with. It's our responsibility (as Christians first) to be the best spokesperson for God that we can truly be.

So yes, you will sometimes be worn, weary and ready to give up, but know that it is part of the journey. These times of trial will strengthen you. It separates those who have a true heart for serving the Lord from those who are merely posturing in leadership for outward appearance.

Whatever you say or do may become a sermon

Often, the experiences between you and your husband, good or bad, in church or life, will be included in one of your his sermons. Let's face it; people love to hear about real experiences. God uses you all of the time, even when you're not in church. In many instances, those experiences will be of benefit to others. You may not even grasp it when the situation has transpired, but it's now part of the testimony of your life in Christ.

Your behavior, whether good or bad, in church or your life, will be used as sermon fodder. I say, "If you were bad enough to do it, don't flinch or cringe when it comes up in his message." There are times when your husband may reveal details of your life or behavior. Don't get angry, don't get upset. Just smile and say, Amen.

Take care when getting counsel

Frequently, people in your life will attempt to give you "common sense advice". This is a lovely thing, but it is not applicable to your particular ministry. In the Bible, the Lord admonishes, For my thoughts are not your thoughts, neither are your ways my ways, saith the Lord (Isaiah 55:8). So, worldly counsel has little place in the church. If there are areas where you are struggling, I advise you seek God in prayer for resolution.

Friends and relatives cannot always properly help you. In fact, you may end up souring them on Christianity if you try to confide in them or seek their help. If you are fortunate enough to meet a long-suffering, experienced, wise PW who is willing to give you counsel, you have hit the spiritual jackpot! Take every bit of advice she gives you. Take notes! Listen intently and soak it all in! You should only receive from those who've walked much longer in the shoes that you're currently in. Consider a connection like this a gift from God.

Getting close to you to get close to the pastor

Beware! There are times when people will befriend you or give you things to get close to your husband. Just as the serpent knew exactly how to tempt Eve, people will use you as a shortcut to get to the pastor. What better way to get their complaints, suggestions, ministerial goals, wants and needs quickly in front of the busy man of God than to run it through his wife? You have your husband's ear all of the time; he values what you say. If he senses it is an important issue, he will listen fully.

Always utilize discretion and discernment when people preface their statements with "Can you ask pastor..." Do not make any promises; encourage them to go to him directly. I tell congregants that I do not act independently of my spouse. If there is a specific request or item that you're looking for, it must go through my husband as God has appointed him head of this church. It is unfair of anyone to ask you to use your wifely influence over your husband to secure ministerial wants, needs, or goals. Draw a firm line, PW, and do not compromise. People will soon realize that you cannot be manipulated.

Jealous much?

The PW must be secure in who she is. You must be so steadfast that you are not easily shaken. Women are attracted to the charismatic men of God. They are attracted to men under the anointing of God preaching dynamically, laying hands on folks and seeing people fall out under God's power. Let's be real: most churches are overflowing with single, lonely women.

Your husband, the pastor, who is charming and engaging (and who looks good in that suit!) can look really attractive to them. He is also a compassionate listener who is there to counsel and advise, and always available to his flock. This can lead to lengthy phone conversations, late night meetings, texts and emails that you aren't privy to. Can you handle that? Even to the point where your husband may be called out of your bed in the middle of the night?

Again, can you handle that? Because you must.

In doing the work of the Lord, your husband does not have time to address your insecurities and petty jealousies. He cannot effectively minister when he feels that you are hurting or upset. If you are taking care of him at home, or plainly speaking, if you are satisfying his sexual appetite, then he won't have a hunger for anything else. A wise woman once said, "What you did to get him, you must do to keep him."

You have to be willing to allow God to use your husband fully while you maintain faith in God and not allow your insecurities to get in the way. The women in the church may, sometimes, feel animosity towards the PW if she acts in a defensive or possessive manner concerning her mate. If your jealousies, anger, or any other emotional detritus filter into the ministerial works of your husband, you need to get some spiritual counsel immediately. It may be nothing more than some time spent in prayer, asking God to reveal the roots of these emotions. If that doesn't work, it may take deliverance ministry to expel these types of spirits that are controlling you.

Women will, sometimes, try to discredit or malign you directly to your husband. They have developed an inordinate affection for your spouse as their pastor and will broadcast your shortcomings to anyone who will listen. You will face the full brunt of their jealousy because, plainly speaking, they are in love with him. I cannot stress the importance of you taking care of your husband.

As I have previously stated: If you are meeting his needs, he does not need to have them met elsewhere. When you got married, your husband chose you; keep that in remembrance if situations such as this arise. We must pray, but as one of our local pastors, John Hannah, says, "There is a time to take off that prayer shawl and put on those heels!" if you don't do it, trust me, there are many waiting for the opportunity. And let's be real: there are numerous women praying for that opportunity. Don't give place to the enemy. You'll ruin your marriage, your family, and your church.

All the single ladies

Don't take it lightly that you have become a role model for the women in the church. They have been watching you. Some may openly model or copy you. Be careful not to encourage such behavior.

Lately, I have had women come to me and say they appreciate seeing me by my husband's side in ministry. They tell me how they enjoy seeing a married couple joyfully serving God together in church leadership positions. They mention how they haven't seen many examples of it done successfully. They also tell me that, one day, they hope to minister alongside their spouse (or future spouse) in ministerial environments.

It is important that you learn how to reach all the women in your church, whether single or married. I believe that you have components to offer all of them. You can use your position as the PW to demonstrate the effectiveness of God's word in real life settings as they see you, interact with you, and are instructed by you.

You will need to learn how to impart and equip these women based on your personal experiences and biblical insight. Allow the Holy Spirit to mold you into what is needed for that spiritual house to impart into those women, both young and old. Do not be hindered or limited by your past experiences. God is using you right now! Pour richly into those who are teachable. For those who are contentious and disagreeable, add them to the top of your prayer list.

She doesn't like me

Some PWs will not win popularity contests. I would be suspicious of those who do! Jesus offended many, and sometimes you will too. Some women will not like you, and there is nothing you can do to change it. No amount of charm or charisma will alter how they may feel. So, what do you do?

We must remember to show love. Love them regardless of how they may feel about you. Use Jesus as your example. On the cross of Calvary, He asked His Father to forgive them "for they know not what they do." Same for you, PW. When we encounter blatant hatred and dislike, we must learn to see past that and look at the human being behind those emotions (demons) and pray for them and show love despite what may be shown to you.

Ministry is not about popularity. If your feelings are getting hurt, you may need to spend more time fasting, praying and gaining deliverance to control the desires of your flesh that yearns to be liked by everyone.

CHAPTER

FOUR

A place called forgiveness

Forgiveness is the oil that turns the wheel of God in our lives. We must liberally apply it to all persons, places and things that cause offense. The adoption of it into our lifestyle changes the way we deal with every single entity that crosses our path. From the person who cuts you off in traffic, to the rude sales clerk, to ministerial hurts and rejections. You hurt God's people when you attempt to minister to them in a state of unforgiveness. You carry the burden that you are supposed to cast on Jesus when you do not forgive. As a PW, all of your past hurts, offenses and setbacks need to be given to the Lord so that He can use you effectively. Forgiveness is the way to accomplish that.

From time to time, it's important to ask God to examine your life. The Lord will show you areas where you are being burdened with things that may be hindering your spiritual growth. Time after time, forgiveness will be at the root of most things that beset you. As a PW, there are many who you will need to forgive, especially those from your past, present, and future. It's a trait that you'll need to keep close as God begins to use you more in His Kingdom.

Bones from the closet

Here you are: this sanctified, mighty woman of God, a leader in the Church, the esteemed pastor's wife. God has cleaned you up well, but out of left field, an incident dredges up from your past. What do you do?

Sometimes, events from our past may show up at your church or on your social media. The women who we are today look nothing like the girls of our past. The Bible says that you will reap what you have sown, so some things are unavoidable. Be not deceived; God is not mocked: for whatsoever a man soweth, that shall he also reap (Galatians 6:7). God's will is sovereign. If you have been honest with your spouse, this surprise should not be a downfall.

If he is unaware, the trust you have built within your marital relationship should be able to absorb the shock of any attack the enemy has launched. This further speaks to the importance of the PW being in proper position. If you are in a correct place, you have a tremendously fortified team on your side to help protect and restore you, if needed. However, if you are operating in a "peacock" spirit, this may be your undoing and could negatively impact the ministry.

This is best handled with honesty because whatever may arise will not exceed God's love for you. Repent, if you have not done so already. Pick yourself up, dust yourself off and keep it moving in Jesus. Many in God's kingdom have speckled pasts and dicey histories. This only speaks to our gratitude for Him "saving a wretch like me" and turning us into new creatures in Christ. His mercies are renewed daily, and He remembers our sin no more. If the congregation is unable to forgive or forget, you're going to have to learn how to minister effectively in the midst of their disapproval.

Appearances count

Okay, in all truthfulness, I've always disliked that the PW has to dress up. You can often immediately spot the First Lady in the room. Seeing her in a J. Renee three piece coordinated bedazzled suit with the matching hat, shoes and Bible cover makes me want to grind my teeth! It reminds me of the Pharisees of the New Testament.

When I first became a PW, I wore the same clothes to church that I wore to work; business-casual. My no-nonsense poly-cotton blends worked fine for me. After all, doesn't God look at our heart instead of our apparel? *...for the Lord seeth not as man seeth; for man looketh on the outward appearance, but the Lord looketh on the heart (1 Samuel 16:7)*. I was able to get away with that for a long time until I got rebuked multiple times.

In the first instance of rebuke, I was told that people would not take me seriously as a leader if I did not dress the part. Even at my job, where the attire is business-casual, you can tell the leader by the stylish clothes they wear. The second instance of rebuke: I was plainly told by a mighty woman of God that my appearance was "not cutting it". She told me that my husband was going places, and as his wife, my choice of wardrobe was unacceptable for the areas that he would be called to go to. She told me that I "needed to do better" and that she would help me to get what was needed to dress appropriately. So, I began to wear formal suits and dresses to church. I felt this was still not befitting of my personality, I then started to refine my wardrobe with more casual types of suits and coordinates, jewelry, and heels. This was a happy medium for me.

In my experiences, PWs who dress plain and dowdy only seem to reinforce a stagnant quality to the ministry. Those who dress youthful and trendy imply a worldliness and desire to compete. Those who dress in an extravagant fashion exhibit a "look at me" spirit that focuses more on themselves than Jesus. Each time I see that, it makes me want to run away in terror.

While it's true that God looks at our hearts and not our outward appearances; we are called to draw men and women to Jesus with the witness of our lives and not our wardrobe. Along with the need to learn and employ good leadership skills, you will need to dress the part to be effective in your ministerial role. I encourage you to find a sense of style that will not overshadow, compete, or interfere with the work you are attempting to accomplish. It should complement, not compete with, your husband's appearance. If your primary function is youth ministry, you will need to dress differently than if your primary function is prison ministry.

Appearance is an area where you can guide your husband if he is struggling with his apparel. Let me say that I haven't seen too many pastors with wardrobe struggles. In the brotherhood of pastorship, they tend to help each other out, but the PWs run the gamut. I've seen it all: from apparel fit for the White House to apparel straight from the crack house! Let's identify it as a struggle; when we know better, we do better. Just as God has cleaned us up from the things we did in the world, He will clean us up to accurately represent His Kingdom. And, sometimes, it comes in the form of a reproof. Learn not to resent those in authority who are striving to help as they reprimand or admonish us.

Allow yourself to be used of God not by God's people

We've all dealt with this: a person comes to the ministry with a terrible story. Everyone (I mean everyone) has done them wrong. From their parents, siblings, relatives, to the world. They've been deemed helpless and hopeless and have no one left to turn to but God. As they become part of the church and part of your life, it's only natural for you to help. You give them your time, talent, and treasure. Soon, you find yourself giving more, much more; job references, deposits for apartments, paying utility bills, buying groceries, cars, etc. (usually from your personal money and not that of the church). This person essentially becomes your personal ministry. You consistently make supreme efforts to restore or elevate them to a place where all their woes cease. It's your sincere desire to get them to a position where they will be able to pay their own bills and keep a job. Sound familiar?

There's an invisible line between helping and enabling. We cannot always see where or when we cross that line. I often have to ask myself, "Am I helping this person to become a better person in Jesus? Or am I enabling this person to continue this cycle in Jesus?" It's a dilemma that requires much discernment and prayer.

There are people, believe it or not, who only join churches to seek what they can get. They will ask for all kinds of things (pay their bills, consignors, loans, etc.). They know the philosophy of Jesus and that His true followers are givers. They've come to fleece the sheep and hustle the shepherd.

There are those with genuine and authentic needs who truly appreciate the help of the ministry and will go on to do mighty works in the name of Jesus. There are also those who will continue to take whatever you give and continuously turn it into what they know. Example: if they have a poverty mentality and you provide them with money, it may disappear quickly with little to show for it. For those types of people, you have become their enabler. You are not helping them.

They know each time they get in trouble that they can tell you their latest sob story and you will acquiesce. They know you will bail them out, supply funds, and come to the rescue. Because. You. Always. Have. As I mentioned previously, there is a significant difference between helping and enabling. Pray to God for discernment to know the difference. Ask Him how you should address such matters so that you do not end up wounding His sheep.

Hold my coat: the improper handling of sheep

In my years as a pastor's wife, I have seen many PWs mishandle the sheep. By mishandling, I mean they are using the sheep for an unintended purpose. Personally, I would love to have a stylist, personal assistant, chauffeur, babysitter, maid, or chef at my fingertips. It would make my life so much easier, but my personal staff should not be totally comprised of the members of God's house.

Many times, the congregants will be eager to help or assist you in any way possible. They love you and your family. They will happily contribute their time and talents to your personal endeavors inside and outside of church if you need them. Is it okay to do this? To take advantage of their kindness and generosity?

Again, I ask you, is it okay to have God's people washing your clothes and doing your grocery shopping? Chauffeuring you around to church services and ministry events in your own car? Mowing your lawn? Watching your kids? Cleaning your house? If they are being paid for their services, this is acceptable; but if they are not, then I call this an improper use of God's people. He sent them to you for guidance and strengthening, not toil and servitude. There is a difference between willful submission and being forced to do things for the pastor and "first lady".

Scripture says God will never give more than you can handle: that includes ministry as well as on the home front. If you are finding yourself overwhelmed, this is not an opportunity to herd God's people and use them as free labor. The members of the church are not your personal entourage. You should not force them to accompany you to events and conferences.

If you are doing this, please stop. As the PW and female lead in your ministry, the women look to you as a role model. They will need guidance as to what they should do in their personal and ministerial lives. We are not meant to be pleasers of men, but pleasers of the Most High God. By forcing others run your errands, you are teaching them to please you rather than the Lord. Besides, you can clean out your own cabinets.

Hit the road, Jack!

It has been prophesied to me many times to go with my husband and travel with him as he ministers across the country. The reason is twofold. First, he can always use my help as he ministers. I am a familiar face in the crowd, a dinner companion, someone who can take care of him and iron his shirt. Secondly, there have been many stories of how extensive travel breeds loneliness and how the enemy can use this as an occasion to insert temptation and opportunities for indiscretion.

Ladies, let's be real! It is not a trust issue. If your husband is hungry and he sees a steak, what is going to happen? I am sure you know the answer to that question. So, find a sitter to watch the kids, get a boarding service for your dog, purchase a nice set of luggage and begin your season of travel ministry. Remember, God has called you both to ministry. As a married couple, you are one in Him. When your husband hits the road, you should too.

Women have come to me after traveling ministry events and told me how they enjoy seeing couples minister together. They've shared their fears and reluctance of doing it, and I encourage them that traveling with their spouse as he ministers is paramount. I stress this; do it as much as allowable, considering your circumstances.

Always have a sermon in your purse

There will come a time when people will want to hear from you. As much as you do or do not desire it, you will be called to minister. Women's events, seminars, Mother's Day, luncheons, etc.; people will begin to call on you. You will have to preach. You will have to teach. You will have to pray for people. You will have to travel.

This cannot be done by sitting in the front row; you'll be required to step into the pulpit. You are not just arm candy for your husband but a vital, supportive role to assist in the success of the ministry. This includes ministering in-house as well as outside of your church. Begin to prepare now. As God gives you revelation in your prayer and worship time, begin to record it in journals and notebooks. Keep notes for sermon ideas or things that drop into your spirit. Start a folder on your computer and begin to write as I did. My husband told me to keep a sermon on "standby" in the event I am called to minister on short notice.

Learn to get comfortable with speaking to groups. Start by teaching and ministering within your own church. Cultivate wisdom in your life. I encourage you to increase your study time in the areas of prayer, deliverance, altar work, healing, prophecy, etc. This will help you tremendously when you step into the pulpit. Yes, we rely on the Holy Spirit, but the Holy Spirit has to have something to work with. Study to shew thyself approved unto God, a workman that needeth not to be ashamed, rightly dividing the word of truth (2 Timothy 2:15).

Your ministry

If you don't know where your personal ministry lies, don't worry, it will be revealed to you. Over time, as you increase in prayer, wisdom, serving the Lord and overall ministerial experience, you will find yourself drawn to a specific calling, whether it involves women's ministry, outreach, children's ministry, hospitality, etc. There are many areas where God will be able to use you effectively as a PW, but one, in particular, will become your personal platform. You will find yourself continuously ministering on this topic, frequently counseling people in this area, and often people will be drawn to you concerning this topic. You will spend much of your free time researching, studying, preparing, and building yourself in this area. You will receive prophetic words concerning this topic.

This, PW, is your personal ministry (the ministry within the ministry). As you have been faithful over another man's work, God has now given you an assignment. When you pray and labor over this work, it's important not to neglect your first love. Keep in mind that your first calling, before the inception of your personal ministry, was to be the pastor's wife. Your dedication to your own ministry should not overshadow your duties as a pastor's wife. Do not abdicate your position during this season as your husband will need your help. The launching of your personal ministry should not be detrimental and disruptive to your church.

God does all things decently and in order. During this time of expansion and elevation for you, remember this Scripture: And we know that all things work together for good to them that love God, to them who are the called according to his purpose (Romans 8:28). So, you must keep things in perspective. Your individual ministry will be fulfilling, exciting, thrilling, and scary at the same time. Bear in mind, it was birthed and refined out of your experience of being the pastor's wife and not a replacement for your original assignment.

Don't be afraid to be yourself

I believe one of the biggest hindrances to a PW is a lack of confidence in showing God's people who we truly are as individuals. We are often afraid to reveal our true selves to God's people. The Lord made you unique. There's no one else like you. Your fingerprints do not match those of any other person on this planet. The corneas of your eyes are not identical to anyone else.

But even the very hairs of your head are all numbered... (Luke 12:7). You are an exceptional and original creation of God and He is not in the cloning business. He is not in favor of you copying someone else. When you seek to pattern your behavior after another person (as I attempted to copy other PWs in the beginning), unless it is Jesus, you are making a terrible mistake. We must understand that God has called us fully to be PWs just as we are. Let me repeat: just as we are. You don't have to do anything special; you don't have to make major alterations. You only need to be yourself and He will do the rest. God does mighty and incredible things through people who are willing and obedient.

Often, we are insecure as we begin to walk in the PW role due to the fact that it is unfamiliar territory. It's extremely plausible that you don't have too many PWs who are willing to give you any advice. You probably have not encountered many people who have been in your shoes. Instead, we have numerous individuals who are quick to judge, condemn, find fault with us or even try to usher us into roles or areas that we don't feel prepared for. Don't let the rigors of ministry change you. Don't let the callous behavior of those in the pulpit harden your heart. Don't allow the self-centered behavior of those who proclaim to be God's anointed turn you away from the true purpose of ministry: to help people in the name of Jesus.

In your role of as a PW, you will see things you don't want to see, hear things you don't want to hear. You may see the lives of notable men and women of God revealed in shocking acts such as theft, indiscretion, malicious intent, lies, robbery and various types of sin. A mighty woman of God once told me that whatever you see, dream, or hear that disturbs you, it is the direction for which you must begin to pray.

You are a powerful woman

You may not realize your power. You are strong. You are amazing. There are many gifts that you have been given that will help you succeed in ministry. God has chosen you specifically for this assignment from the foundation of the world. The call is great, but the temptation is great as well. You are called to submit. You are not called to control.

Be wise and keep God's heart in everything you do. It is only His Will that enables us to endure and persevere in the work of the ministry. The power that you have in your marital relationship with your husband cannot be used to control him in a ministerial setting. The Bible says women are to submit to their own husbands. Meaning that all the power that you have, all the might you feel coursing through your veins should fall under the authority of your husband.

Wives, submit yourselves unto your own husbands, as unto the Lord (Ephesians 5:22).

When you decide to act in your own strength, you are no different than Eve in the Garden. She moved into a position of dominance that was solely designated for Adam (her husband). Take Eve's disastrous example to heart so that you do not end up in a similar situation. Yes, we are modern women in a modern society, but God has designated a specific order for His purpose and glory.

A mighty man of God once said, "Submission is never weakness; it's simply power under control." Take that to heart, PW. Power-Under-Control. Take your God-given power and authority, and submit it to your husband. Fully. Don't listen to the single ladies; don't listen to the advice of the feminists and women's libbers when doing the work of ministry. I repeat: In God's Kingdom, there is a specific order for His purpose and glory.

Let not your heart be hardened

Over the years my husband and I have been used, mistreated, lied about, back-stabbed, ghosted, maligned, etc. This has been done by people we have ventured to help in the name of Jesus. This situation is quite normal for those who work in ministry.

These scenarios often cause me to create a protective coating around my emotions and feelings, hoping to prevent being wounded in the future.

During these times I became more callous, losing some compassion for others. I find that I am focusing more on myself and my personal circumstances, often drifting into a depressive emotional state. When I begin to realize what has happened, I immediately war in the Spirit and pray to get that demon off of me. I ask Jesus Christ to restore my heart, to remove the cold darkness and return it to a heart like His. We cannot become so fearful of being hurt that we shut people out and shut down when painful situations occur.

Jesus is the Healer. God cannot fully use you for His purpose when you are afraid to give Him access to every area of your life so that He can use it for His Glory. When we are hurt, instead of closing Him out, we should turn the issue over to Him so that we may be restored and healed. It's vital that we not allow these types of things to penetrate our ability to properly minister to and help those in need. Know that, yes, you may get hurt or injured along the way, but look at the lives of the disciples and the early Christians. The lives of these "sold out" men and women of God were filled with grim and frightful situations.

Many of us do not experience outward persecution, but as I have previously mentioned, ministry is challenging, and we must not let people or situations turn us into heartless automatons. The Bible promises us that God will never leave or forsake us.

Let your conversation be without covetousness; and be content with such things as ye have: for he hath said, I will never leave thee, nor forsake thee (Hebrews 13:5).

O LORD my God, I cried out to You, and you healed me (Psalm 30:2).

God promises us healing and restoration. Don't allow people to cause you to lose your joy in serving the Lord. Remember your first love and allow God to renew and revitalize you in the midst of pain, hardship, and adversity.

CHAPTER

FIVE

Leading the women

How do you relate to the females in your congregation as a PW? This is an area where I struggle. In the beginning, I treated the women as friends. We would talk on the phone, go to lunch, laugh, joke, and have a good time. I was having fun.

That was wrong. Why? Because I had befriended them and we were pals. When the time came for me to be a leader, they didn't respect me as such because they didn't see me as an authority figure; instead, they saw me as a peer. As a matter of fact, I didn't even see myself as a person in charge. I didn't have enough confidence to believe that I could lead them. Truthfully, I did not want to lead them. I wanted to continue to have fun and dodge my responsibilities in the ministry.

I was unable to counsel them because I didn't operate in authority and thus, they weren't able to receive from me. Thus, my actions negatively affected my husband's pastoral role. The women of the church didn't have a willing female leader to pray and counsel with, so they turned to him for the things they needed. This, in effect, caused him to perform double duty. He ultimately had to counsel everyone, men and women, because I was not in the proper position to minister to the female members of the church. Some female members of the church only want to talk with another woman. They love and honor the pastor, but they need accessibility to his wife to get the things they need concerning wisdom and counsel from a feminine perspective.

There were also certain women I met who would try to push me into a dominant role. They would tell me things to say to my husband. They would say that I needed to be more assertive, "telling" him what to do instead of asking his approval. Some would add that they wouldn't put up with certain things and that I needed to force him to do things in ministry as well as our personal lives. Each time I heeded their voices, it would start a big argument between my husband and I. It brought a spirit of confusion into our relationship. I've since learned that this is a manifestation of the spirit of Jezebel that attempts to prompt the wife to overrule and boss her husband around. Now, I've learned to not adhere to those types of voices. Believe me, there are women who still come to me in that manner, thinking they are helping me to become more assertive.

I do not feel the need to domineer over the women of the church. They see me leading by submitting fully to my husband. The spirit of Jezebel hates that. It will manifest and lash out at you because you defer to your husband. So, what's the best thing that you can do? The more Jezebel manifests and lashes out, the more you submit. Eventually, submission wins. This spirit doesn't feel comfortable in a house where true submission is present. It will eventually drive the spirit out.

In 2013, my husband conducted leadership training, and he asked me to participate. After successfully completing the training, he said that I would be ordained as a pastor in our ministry. I had no desire to walk in the pastorate, but he countered that he wanted me to assume a position of authority with the women in the ministry. This is a prime example of my husband needing me to perform a task that requires that I come out of my comfort zone. I already disliked being addressed as "First Lady" and now I would have to be called "Pastor"? I balked.

He counseled me privately, instructing me on how he wanted me to lead and direct the women of the church. Again, I resisted. He got upset, declaring that he needed my help with the women in the church and I needed to step up. At this point, he'd been pastoring for nearly thirteen years, and I'd been avoiding my ministerial duties for most of that time. He quoted a few scriptures and reminded me for the umpteenth time to submit as the Bible states.

Instead of being the model of passivity that I was, he wanted me to become more active and assertive. His desire was that I galvanize the women and lead them toward victorious living. Wow! Was I supposed to do all of that? How was I going to achieve this? Take into account, the women who were part of the ministry did not respect me as a leader because I did not act like one. Each time that I attempted to lead, they didn't respond well. So, I failed in that area, and to this day, I continue to struggle.

I find it difficult to lead the women, but that does not excuse me from the responsibility. At times, there's catty, petty fighting between them. Honestly, it reminds me a lot of being back in high school. It's tough navigating scenarios with women whose feelings get hurt easily or those who become offended. They are grown women, not teenagers! Yet these types of circumstances cause division among church members and prevent us from being effective in our primary assignment, which is to demonstrate the love of Jesus.

What does one do? I'm no expert in women's leadership.

"Keep it real" is my personal mantra. I'm a real woman, with a real life and a real heart for Jesus. I have real struggles as every person does. I make mistakes, and I'm constantly looking for solutions.

I feel that it is best if you put a bit of space between yourself and the female members of the church. Yes, you read that correctly; I am saying it is best not to get too close. Familiarity breeds contempt, and this has happened to me numerous times. PW, the women of the church are not meant to be your BFFs, girl squad, or entourage. If you desire to be a leader be one, not a buddy. If you don't, they will not respect you or follow you.

You cannot do the same things they do. You cannot always go places with them to have fun. If you desire to lead, that must be your decision at all times. Is it fun? No, but it's not about you or what you want to do. It's about the mandate God has placed upon your life to lead His people. You are on assignment.

We must have the posture of a leader. You should envision yourself as one. You must act and think like a forerunner. If you are struggling in that capacity, pray! Get some books on leadership qualities. More importantly, your husband, the pastor, is the head of the church. I am quite sure he is already overflowing with amazing leadership skills. Begin to glean from him. Ask him how and what you should be doing to benefit the women in your church.

Trust God above all, no matter what happens

I can tell you from the experience of sitting in the emergency room at 3:00 am with three little kids that you must completely place your trust in God. Your encounters in ministry will be some of the most thrilling, terrifying, amazing, horrifying, overflowing, and desolate times. I think you're getting the idea of where I'm going with this, correct?

You will undergo great highs and lows. Your faith will be tried, stretched, and developed. Each area of your life is open and transparent as God uses you and your husband in ministry. You have to learn to fully rely on Him for everything because He has called you. The Lord has gotten you to this point and will be with you every step of this journey. His word tells us that He'll never leave nor forsake us, even in the depths of hell, He is Emmanuel (God is with us).

I have been shocked by the lack of empathy I've seen in the body of Christ. The backbiting and underhanded behavior that emanates from some pulpits is unbelievable. Seeing these types of behaviors caused me to question God initially until He began to show me that I needed to trust Him completely. He is the Just Judge, Final Authority, Alpha and Omega, and all I need to do is submit and obey Him. He will take care of the rest. I am Alpha and Omega, the beginning and the ending, saith the Lord, which is, and which was, and which is to come, the Almighty (Revelation 1:8).

We must pray for our enemies and pray for those who despitefully use us. Additionally, we must pray without ceasing (1 Thessalonians 5:17). God can and will work miracles, through us in this earthly realm. First and foremost, we must be willing and obedient. Secondly, we must trust without question, believe without seeing, and have no fear. The fact that God has called you and your husband to ministry is a great honor, one that should never be taken lightly. In Matthew 22:14 Jesus stated that, "For many are called, but few are chosen." He's chosen you because He knows that you can do it. The enemy recognizes the same thing, and that's why you are challenged. If God is your constant counsel, at no time will you ever go wrong.

Take this job and shove it!

As I write this, my husband and I are both working regular

(sometimes referred to as "secular") full-time jobs in addition to our ministerial duties. When we first started the ministry, the church was small and didn't require as much of our personal time as it does now. The more members in the congregation, the more will be required of you. I've heard of quite a few pastors telling their members that God has called them to ministry full-time. They quit their jobs, and begin what's often referred to as the "Sunday-press", where tithes and offerings are used as battering rams. The requests for love gifts and pastoral offerings become more frequent. Most of the congregants are hounded to financially support the ministry so that the pastor can be free to do the Lord's work.

Scripture calls the Lord Jehovah-Jireh (Yahweh will provide) in the book of Genesis. If your ministerial burden affects your ability to work a regular job, then you will need to devote much time and prayer to determine if full-time ministry is your portion. It's a blessing to be free to do the Lord's work full-time. For the majority of us in the service of the Lord, we'd love to be able to do it starting tomorrow! If your ministry is unable to provide health benefits and a regular salary, it is important that you truly count the cost before abandoning your secular vocation. Your lifestyle will have to change considerably in order to accommodate this leap of faith. If you have children, you have to keep them in mind (especially young children). There should be a weighing of the costs of cutting back on certain household luxuries versus the freedom of being a God chaser.

Immunizations, college funds, braces, broken bones, child care: these types of things become mountains instead of molehills when you don't have a consistent paycheck and corporate benefits. You never, ever want to find yourself ministering for money. When your children begin to connect the shortcomings in their lives that correspond directly to your fervency with God, it may cause resentment to build in them if not handled properly. As mentioned previously, if in my desire to serve Jesus I turn my kids away from Him, I have failed.

So, it's a conundrum: wanting the freedom to serve God in the way you're led and not wanting to shackle the ministry with supporting your household. We should not limit God and His ability to do great and mighty things in our lives. It is also true that God has given us a brain to use. He desires that we move in wisdom and not in our own anxiousness to jump into full-time ministry. Most importantly, it looks really bad when you said God told you to quit your job and you find yourself dusting off your resume a year later to begin a job search.

To your health!

Most pastors I know start their ministries while working regular jobs. They use personal monies to purchase and pay for things like site rental fees, equipment and whatever is required to start the church. Most will have to build membership over time, having confidence in God to send those sheep to fill the pews. People who will give of their time, talent, and treasure, to increase the impact and scope of the ministry. Things that are planted in good soil will germinate when properly watered and fed. The same will happen in ministry as God provides the people, while you and your husband supply the proper environment.

However, there's a physical and mental toll that impacts those in church leadership, especially the pastor. As his wife, you have to make sure that he maintains his health and decreases his stress levels. There is nothing more traumatic than dealing with a bunch of murmuring and complaining saints who tend to find fault in things said and done by their leader (ask Moses). There are those who will nit-pick and overthink sermons, looking for themselves in any chastisement or rebuke, leading them to seek an audience with the pastor on a regular basis. There are others who will use their membership and/or offering as a tool to control the pastor, threatening to leave if certain things are not done according to their requests.

Troublemakers. Demon possessed. Disgruntled. Crazy. These are some of the characteristics leaders of the local church have to deal with on a daily basis. Did you hear me? Daily basis! As social media has increased, the ability for congregants to have access to the pastor has become virtually unlimited, especially if he participates as well. While this pastor is working his secular job, he's getting texts, phone calls, Facebook messages, Tweets, Instagrams, Snapchats, and more, concerning church and spiritual matters. In the past, leaders would get breaks between services, but today's pastors barely get breaths between having to be of service.

So, yes, it is, at times, stressful. That is why it is so important for the PW to be in the proper position to assist her husband in certain ministerial duties. At the same time, in our personal lives, we have to keep the pastor healthy. PW's need to make sure he eats right since most pastors I know have terrible diets (lots of fast food, fried chicken, junk foods, too much sugar and soda). They don't get enough exercise, sleep, or relaxation time. To make matters worse, the pastor spends so much time caring for others; he'll rarely go to the doctor concerning his own health. He'll ignore physical symptoms and warnings until it is almost too late.

Yes, I know you're busy with kids, work, and ministry. It's a lot for one woman to handle. However, you only have one husband, and he needs your help. It is not easy to get him to eat vegetables, decrease sugar and junk foods, but you must keep patiently suggesting and providing nutritious alternatives that promote good health.

Controlling dietary choices is difficult, but you can help him decrease stress. This can be accomplished by making sure he gets regular checkups and keeps scheduled appointments with a physician. These tend to be the first things canceled during his busy schedule. Help him work through challenges and be a listening ear when he needs to talk things through and gain perspective. Assist him by keeping the stress levels low in your household and encourage times for respite, replenishment and recreation. Since we're wives here, we know the biggest stress buster is sex. Eating can sometimes turn into a substitute for a healthy sex life between a married couple. I've seen far too many fat, grouchy pastors. When I witness that PW, I'm looking at you.

There will be times when you feel as if you are about to lose your mind concerning ministerial issues. Sometimes, you may feel the need to seek outside counsel. I think one of the biggest shortcomings in contemporary Christendom is the lack of providing a Christian based program to deal with mental health for those in need. You may need to speak with a professional relating to situations going on in your life. Choose wisely in order to assure that you will receive counsel from an individual who will give you a perspective concerning your mental health that's in line with God's word. We are quick to suggest prayer as a resolution to problems, but for some, prayer may need to be in tandem with a visit to a Christian counselor.

Take care of your health physically and mentally. Sometimes, we need some perspective, a safe place to vent, and possibly some outside help. Don't be afraid to do this for yourself. If you are experiencing troubling issues, they may filter into your ministry. There can also be a potential transference of spirits when you lay hands on people. Simply meaning, the spirits (instability, anger, etc.) that have gotten on you may get on the individual that you're putting your hands on. It is like the precious ointment upon the head, that ran down upon the beard, even Aaron's beard: that went down to the skirts of his garments (Psalm 133:2). So, do not discount the need to be mentally restored so that God can continue to use you in ministry.

Those ain't Bebe's kids...they belong to the pastor

Unfortunately, the pastor's kids (PK's, as they are lovingly called) get a bad reputation. I've had one church member tell me to my face that the pastor's children are the worst behaved kids in the church! I struggled not to get offended, as I was certain she was disrespecting my children.

PK's are in church a lot (too much, if you ask some of my relatives). Nonetheless, because of the work of their parents, they attend many more services and church events than most adults will experience in a lifetime. They know they must behave, sit still for very long periods of time, and forgo playtime, snacks, and beverages until the work of the Lord is completed.

It's easy when they're younger. As they get old enough to understand the difference between their lives versus the lives of their peers, it's more challenging to keep them occupied in church without them being disruptive. And because PK's are more comfortable in church settings, they are usually the first ones to "show out", as we say.

Train up a child in the way he should go: and when he is old, he will not depart from it (Proverbs 22:6). I believe the word of God my that children hear is being stored somewhere in their brain cells and will benefit them in the future. This will most certainly provide a godly foundation for their lives that my husband and I did not receive as children. At times, their behavior will test and try me in church settings. I attempt to minimize their distracting behaviors so that my husband can minister without having to reprimand them. Keep in mind that many of the church members are scrutinizing your kids. Their appearance, wardrobe (or lack thereof), behavior, attitude are noted, and most people will feel free to express their opinions to you. They will rarely come to the pastor with this foolishness, just his wife.

Twenty years from now, I may no longer remember the name of the woman who said my children behaved badly. I will most certainly have three grown women who've spent a good portion of their formative years going to church and watching their father preach and teach God's word. I want them to love God. My current aspiration is not to be so stringent with their behavior in church, but to be more concerned with their spiritual development. I need to make sure they understand realness and relationship with God and not solely the boring rote of church attendance.

So, what am I saying? It's not about your kids being perfectly packaged and sitting in rapt attention. I've encountered far too many PK's now grown up who resent their parents for making them go to church, and who, by choice, deny God in their lives. At the same time, the church is not a jungle gym or play yard with your kids leading the way in misbehaving. Balance is key; the Bible says, A false balance is abomination to the LORD: but a just weight is his delight (Proverbs 11:1). As PWs, we have to keep a close eye on our children, not merely to note their behaviors in God's house, but to see God's house in their behavior.

It's a family affair

So how does one keep their family intact in the midst of this type of lifestyle? I often tell people that "ministry eats marriages". The rigors of pastoring and leading God's people will impact many areas of your life. You are the one who is responsible for keeping balance, order, and sanity within your household.

Let's start with your marriage. You must sow back into your relationship. Institute date nights and spend time with your husband purely having fun. Find an activity that you both will enjoy, try to reconnect back the carefree times you had in the past to momentarily de-stress and just enjoy each other's company. Try not to discuss church issues when it's your time alone with your husband. It's hard, I know! You both deserve a much-needed break—and you won't get too many of them, so try to enjoy yourself.

In regards to the children, I need to reiterate that it was simpler when they are younger. They were easily corralled and entertained in church settings, and got used to lengthy services. Often my purse was filled with toys, candy, and crayons so the children could amuse and entertain themselves in the back rows during services. As they have gotten older in the midst of this electronic age, they spend much of their time playing with cellphones and other electronic devices when not participating in Children's Church. These days our kids are more vocal concerning church attendance and will often say angrily, "We have to go to church again?" when we attend services outside of our own.

My children are just now approaching the preteen years, so I have yet to experience the tests of making teenagers and young adults attend church. I will tell you that it is a challenge that I've seen some leaders deal with successfully and unsuccessfully. It is far more critical that you realize that you are a mother before you are a "First Lady". We must parent our children within God's guidelines and not use church or ministry as a bargaining tool. Our children should want to have a personal relationship with God outside of anything that we have done. It is our primary assignment to ensure that our children grow up to be adults who love the Lord and have a desire to serve Him.

I used to force my children to sing in the kid's choir, ignoring and overriding their complaints and desire not to do so. One Sunday, as I watched my oldest daughter purposely standing mute in front of the congregation as my other two robotically performed the song I'd made them practice in the car repeatedly, I decided that enough was enough. No longer would I push them or guilt trip them if they didn't want to participate. It has been hard for me to do this; at times, I relapse back to "Sanctified Tiger Mom" and force them to praise dance. I am determined to stop.

There have been numerous instances when we'll visit a church where the pastor's kids are playing instruments, singing, and doing many types of things. My heart leaps when I see this! I would love for my children to do that. Realistically, I remind myself simply to be happy that they are all physically in the church.

Battlin' Jezebel

Over the years, I've had scores of run ins with the spirit of

Jezebel in our church. Sometimes I've prevailed, and other times that spirit has gotten the best of me. I thought, incorrectly, that once we got "her" out of the church "she" would never return. I couldn't understand why we had to keep battling Jezebel over and over again. We battle this spirit; it's gone for a season (period of time), and there is peace. It comes again after a time and we have to start the same process over again.

One day, I was so exasperated from dealing with Jezebel, and I asked God why. The response I received from the Holy Spirit was quite interesting. He instructed me to study the spirit and to examine the nature of the spirit. The nature or name denotes its purpose. What was the primary focus and aim of Jezebel in scripture? When you learn the purpose, you will learn the assignment of that spirit. As I studied, I found that the purpose of Jezebel was to usurp the power of those in authority and to silence prophetic voices.

The Holy Spirit further revealed that until that spirit has accomplished those goals in our ministry, it would continue to come. Just as Jesus was led into the wilderness to be tempted for a period of time, the same may happen to us. I am part of a prophetic ministry, so the prophetic voice rings loud and true in our church, and the spirit of Jezebel despises that. Therefore,

I would have to learn to fight and defeat this spirit at each manifestation.

These days, I have gotten pretty adept at identifying Jezebel when she walks in the door. When that person decides to join the ministry I have to be very careful about how I interact with them because Jezebel has now decided to become a member as well.

Some of the things I've learned about the spirit of Jezebel include:

- Often, the spirit of Ahab will manifest prior to the appearance of Jezebel. You must pay attention. When Ahab is in the building, Jezebel is often very close. Do not miss this warning. Being forewarned enables you to be forearmed. Sometimes, Jezebel will try to hide, but Ahab is the companion spirit needed for Jezebel to manifest.

- Jezebel attempts to draw close to the leaders. She will often quickly befriend them, sometimes giving expensive gifts and/or large monetary gifts to win favor. She will initially be very enthusiastic and supportive of the ministry, exhorting things that she will do and talents she will use to help, often highlighting past achievements in other ministries.

- Jezebel will often befriend the lonely PW. Zeroing in on commonalities, she will align herself to become a confidante of the PW, gaining access to areas of weakness where the PW may struggle.

- Subtlety is key! Slowly, over time, Jezebel's manipulations will come to the surface. There is usually a continual clash between this spirit and the other women in the church. You will often find yourself being the mediating party because of things she has said or done.

- This spirit will have large emotional expressions and outbursts: crying, intense rage/anger, or even an almost manic type of joy. This is used to manipulate. These emotional flights can arise quickly and sometimes seemingly on cue.

- She will attempt to infiltrate your marriage, asking pointed questions concerning the working relationship between you and your spouse. She will never really offer advice, but rather say, "If that were me, I wouldn't put up with that."

For many years, I believed the best response to Jezebel was to get her out quickly before major damage occurred. My husband made me begin to look at this spirit differently. He said, "Often the Jezebel is a hurting soul, and we as Christians should try to get that person set free instead of kicking them out."

And God may have assigned that man (yes, it can be in a man too) or woman to your ministry so you can help them to be restored. I've heard Christians sometimes menacingly label women as Jezebel, pronouncing it almost as if it were a curse word over that woman's life. Actually, Jezebel is a demonic spirit that existed long before its namesake appeared on the scene in 1 Kings 16.

The best ways I've found to deal with Jezebel are:

- Do not accept the gifts! They may be timely and much needed, but you must learn to say no.

- Be careful when talking about personal matters with her – do not let your guard down. Keep your conversations biblical and scriptural. This allows little room to divulge personal matters that allow an inroad to your marriage.

- Keep an eye on that person. Watch them around other members of the church. Learn how to effectively mediate any interpersonal issues to not cause offense to either party.

- Submit to your husband! Tell him who you think is manifesting the Jezebel spirit and listen to his advice. Let her see you fully submitted to your husband at all times. If she notices you slipping, she will take advantage of it because she is watching you closely. Remember the serpent and Eve? The snake spoke to her in lieu of her husband, Adam. You are the shortcut to the one in authority.

Most importantly, realize that this person is one of God's children. They need love, healing, and restoration just as we all do. It's your responsibility to make them feel accepted and part of your Christian family; highlight and encourage their strengths and pour into them as much as they will allow.

Frequently the individual will not be able to stay in this type of environment unless they are willing to allow God to change them. Most will leave quickly, but for those that remain, shower them with love and keep your eye on them. Outward manifestations may vary, but if you know the nature, you will easily recognize the attempt of the enemy to infiltrate by this spirit.

The First Man?

I've been to several ministries where the wife is so active in the church that she overshadows her husband. Her role is so prominent that she acts like the pastor and he sits humbly at her side as her willing servant. She's bossing every person in the ministry around, including him!

Personally, I find this hard to stomach. I have yet to see a ministry that functions well when the PW is usurping the authority of her husband. Take care, women! I once heard a bishop say that a pastor's biggest struggle is wanting to be like God. The power of being in the pulpit (elevated above the people), speaking authoritatively to the masses, along with feeling the Holy Spirit surge through their bodies, can corrupt those not strongly rooted and grounded in the foundation of Jesus Christ.

PWs, as you begin to find your place in the ministry, you must remember who God has put in charge over His house. You are the pastor's wife, not the pastor. You cannot and should not override your husband's authority at church in front of the membership. You can discredit the ministry by attempting to control or take over a situation, even if you think you are right in doing so. Again, as God once told me, "You may cause the ministry to fail if you don't submit to your husband."

Can I get a redo?

If I had an opportunity to do it over again, what would I do differently? At this point, I would not say, "I wouldn't change a thing." No, sir! If I had to do it again, there are so many things I'd do differently because, in truthfulness, I had to repent several years ago. I told God I was sorry because I believed that some of my actions or inactions hindered the progress of the ministry.

Fellow PWs, don't make the same mistakes I did. Granted, it could've been worse, but I believe that we would've been so much farther along had I been in the correct position initially. Never underestimate the placement and positioning of the woman in God's plan. When that woman is out of place, absent, deferring, or avoiding her responsibilities, every person involved suffers because of it. There are many references in the Bible that illustrate this point; look at Eve and Sarah. They are examples of women causing problematic things to happen because they did not get along with the vision.

Looking back on my experience, here's what I'd do differently: when we first started the ministry, I was clearly not ready. That was completely my own fault. As I like to say, God will give us warnings before things happen in our lives. Much of the time, we are not paying attention to those warnings. When He brings you into your assignment, He has already armed and prepared you for it.

Before my husband began to pastor, I received many prophetic words about being a pastor's wife. I selfishly chose to ignore them, thinking I had more time or that it would go away because it was an undertaking that I did not want to do. I now realize that God was using people to give me timely information that was needed during my season of preparation. Instead of taking advantage of that time, I turned it into my season of avoidance. There was spiritual and natural work that needed to be done with those words that were being prophetically loosed upon my life at that time.

Spiritually, I should've begun to "war over" the words received and intercede with God so that I would have been better prepared to run with the vision when it began to manifest. Naturally, I should've begun to research and draw from real life inspirations to bolster and fortify myself for the time of application. Because of the fact that I did not do any of those things, I was running from my assignment and continued to run as the vision began to manifest. As a result, I was ill equipped to handle the assignment. I dropped the ball, both spiritually and naturally.

I should've started to look at those around me who were PWs more seriously. I only focused on their negative traits and characteristics, because, remember, I didn't want to do it. Negativity reinforces our desires not to do certain things. Everyone couldn't have been wrong and it was likely that they weren't as bad as I've made them appear. I've come to believe that God surrounds us with people for certain reasons, and it is up to us to find out why.

By focusing only on their undesirable characteristics, I wasn't able to see PWs who could've helped me to not be so jaded and shortsighted. I can guarantee that God placed people in my path those many years ago who would've been good resources, yet I was unable to make the proper connection with them because I was out of alignment. I most certainly made contact with PW's, but again, being out of position caused me not to interact with them in the divinely appointed manner. It is similar to having one of your fingers popped out of its joint; it's going to be hard to use that finger until it's popped back into the correct position.

As long as I evaded the responsibilities and ignored God's call, I short-sheeted the ministry. God needed both the man and woman in the proper location and alignment with His word and vision, so that He could prosper His work. I was deficient in perspective and prayer. I was just plain selfish! To complicate matters further, I kept having my own personal pity party, murmuring and complaining, only thinking of myself, always asking, "Why me?"

I never thought about how my husband felt. Who was reassuring him concerning his calling besides the Holy Spirit? Was he uncertain pertaining to the task God had given him? Why wasn't I more like the woman in Proverbs 31, praying over my household? The world was against my husband, and even his wife wasn't supporting or covering him in prayer as we began this endeavor. Do you understand now why I had to repent? God's grace covered me even though I was wrong. Don't make the same mistakes that I did. Embrace the vision God has given your husband and run with it. Harvest both the good and bad from those around you; learn from the bad and use the good as building blocks for your role as a PW.

Finally, I had no confidence. What's important to take away from reading this book is that it's okay for us not to have confidence. It's a human trait and often we are unsure, uncertain or hesitant concerning ourselves, our roles and actions. It is understandable that I had no assurance in myself, but I also had no confidence in God, which is the worst part. God chose me. The fact that He selected me demonstrates His faith in me, and that should overshadow and cover any insecurities that may manifest in my mind.

My inability to move in God's confidence and to dwell within my own insecurities gave place to the enemy. Is this sounding familiar? Because it should. Each woman in the Bible who fell prey to the enemy operated within the same spectrum. A treacherous trick of the enemy, yet we continue to be deceived by Satan in this arena, even to this day.

Break this chain, PW; by not allowing it happen to you! It's like Peter walking on water in Matthew 14; when he looked around and became aware of his human limitations, and as fear took over his mind, he began to sink. It was only when he kept his eyes on Jesus that he was able to do the impossible. Having Jesus to focus on in the midst of chaos will allow you to walk over tumultuous water (trouble) that you have no idea how to tread in.

Couples ministry

In 2011, at one of our conferences, I had the honor to watch couples' ministry in action in a way that I'd never seen before. The man of God, an Apostle, delivered a powerful sermon, and then he began to pray for the people and lay hands on them. As he did so, his wife rose from her seat in the audience and joined him on stage, moving powerfully under the anointing. I stood in the back of the room transfixed. She moved like a lioness on the stage, laying hands, praying, people falling out under the anointing.

Both she and her husband, synchronized in the Holy Spirit, flowed in tandem under God's Power. What a sight! I had never seen anything like it before and have not seen it since. It was so awesome! I told her so once it was over. It was impressive. Later that evening my husband told me that he wanted me to do the same thing. ★Gulp★ There was an audible gasp to my reaction. I have no words for what I was thinking. "Shell-shocked" is an adequate adjective to describe what I felt at the time.

Just when you think you have made much progress, here comes another shove to push you outside of your comfort zone. I am most content and comfortable in the background. When I am called to the forefront, there is reticence and an internal struggle that I must contend with because my first inclination is to "work behind the scenes". In my experience as a PW, most people do not want to see me working in the background or sitting by idly, but as a dynamic partner in ministry. It was not my desire to stand behind the pulpit; I thought I'd only be required to be a "good ministry wife". It takes more than that as a PW these days in the contemporary Christian church.

Women see themselves in you and they want you to be well rounded and able-bodied in all ministerial functions. They want to see you preaching, teaching, ministering, and laboring in the same way they too want to serve alongside their spouse. In the past, the First Lady sat in the first row, adorned and arrayed in the picture of beauty, grace, and elegance. Today, the PW sits next to her husband, alert, assisting, ready to jump in like a bench player at an NBA game. You never know when you'll be called, and you have to be ready.

Your approval rating

Are you concerned with what others may think of you? Your answer should always be no. As a PW, you must learn how to obey God, whatever the cost. Many times, the PW is not the most well-liked person, but is popular because of her husband. I never tire of observing how people begin to treat me differently once they find out who my husband is.

While I was previously overlooked or ignored, when they become aware that I'm a PW, their attitude towards me begins to visibly change. They become more careful about what they say or do, will extend courtesies and give special preferences to me that I didn't ask for. In some cases, the opposite will occur; they will become a bit sterner or take out their frustrations with the church on me because I am a PW. It is unfortunate that these types of things happen, but it's far more important to realize that your reaction, while in the midst of these types of situations, is what God is focusing on.

We cannot control how others perceive us. Their misperceptions will color their interactions with us as the PW. They will stereotype us and begin to treat us in a certain manner. We can either acquiesce or use it as an opportunity to prove them wrong. It's best not to react to these types of situations in a prideful manner but merely show love to all, which is what Jesus would do.

God will use anyone at any time to deliver a word in due season. Regardless of how you feel, you are still a minister of the gospel. You just happen to be the PW. Primarily, you are a child of the King and will need to push past any approvals or disapprovals that are directed to you. We should not think more highly of ourselves than we ought to. Instead, humility must remain in the forefront at all times. Again, it doesn't matter what you think, what others may think, or what the congregants think. What is important is what God thinks concerning you. Above all, people must see Jesus in you and receive Him as Lord of their lives without basing it on their approval or disapproval of you as a PW.

Armor-bearer: the right to bear arms?

I'm about to step on some toes right now. I do not believe in armor bearing for modern day Christians. This practice was seen solely in the Old Testament. It was to guard and protect leaders. Fast forward to today, and it has been translated in our churches to one who carries your Bible, your water, drives you around, and pretty much serves as your spiritual and physical butler while you minister or attend events.

In reading through the New Testament, one does not see where Jesus or His disciples were required to bear one another's armor. In fact, they didn't carry armor and neither do we. So why does the PW need an individual to tote her possessions when she's able to do it herself? There's nothing wrong with having a church member who volunteers to assist you by carrying some of your belongings, but to create a specific appointed position in your ministry for such responsibilities reeks of pageantry. This feeds into the stereotype of the First Lady being a high maintenance diva when we see her being waited on like she is some type of foreign dignitary.

As the spiritual mother of your church, you are called to raise up strong daughters, not subordinate aides. I have a house full of daughters, but I ask for assistance instead of demanding servitude. Believe it or not, a person can respect and honor you without a requirement of them carrying your bags or being your plus-one at a women's conference. We may carry babies in our wombs, newborns in bulky carriers, and toddlers strapped to our backs. God forbid if there's an instance when the PW is seen carrying her own purse and tote bag at the same time! What kind of sense does that make? We need to learn how to bear our own armor and not compel others to assist us.

Part of your assignment in ministry is to be a strong support to your husband and become the vessel that God called you to be. If you look at the construction of a building, the materials providing support are often made of stronger material than the structure itself (i.e., concrete foundations supporting a wooden house frame) and the same applies to you. God created woman to be a support (helpmeet). He pulled the wife from an area of support (the side), and has endowed us with the qualities needed to help our husbands in ministry. Like a Swiss army knife, you are constructed with multiple tools nestled inside of you to complete any task that will arise in your church. So, it's not about armor bearing, but bearing arms. Don't look for people to help you, just grab your spiritual weapons and move forward!

Where's the complaint department?

Whenever I have a dilemma, I usually find myself turning to the Lord in prayer for solace and guidance. For example, if my husband does something that I don't like, the first thought I have after working to conquer the anger that arises is to seek counsel. I want to talk to someone. I want to rage, complain and lash out against the wrong that I've felt he has done to me!

As I continue to seethe with the fury, frustration and other emotions that come into play I cycle through my list of possible people who I can talk to. Imagining their conversations with me, avenging myself and complaining about the things my husband does that I don't like. In essence, I'm gaining the upper hand by manipulating my audience with the "why me" stance and sob stories of how difficult my life is because of what has been done. Hearing my confidant cluck disapprovingly on the phone, basically sympathizing with me, bolsters my wounded position by saying, "Yes, you poor dear."

The Holy Spirit will check me, asking what purpose would it serve. Why would I expose my marital issues to a person who would use them as fodder to disrespect my husband? Has he committed an act so terrible that it requires me to stoop to orchestrate a personal pity party to have another human to pacify me? Is it, indeed, so terrible that I need to resort to this manner? Guess what happens next? The wisdom, love, and compassion of God will move upon me, even in my state of anger. I am reminded as God has told me to "cover my husband as Noah's sons covered him". I am assured by the Holy Spirit that God loves me, and this small inconvenience that has arisen is not bigger than His will for our lives. In avenging my wounded ego, am I willing to defraud the very work of Jesus? If I call certain people and tell them my woes, won't they begin to lose respect for my husband? And isn't he a man of God? So, when things happen that you don't like, instead of lashing out, pray. If your husband was truly wrong, God is going to handle it. But if you were wrong, He's coming your way.

What do I do now?

As a PW, I have made many mistakes. I continue to make mistakes. Sometimes, I get in trouble. I get rebuked. I get scriptures quoted to me by my husband to remind me what I am supposed to be doing. This book may not be a perfect representation of my role as PW, and I am not totally unbiased. What I am giving to you in sharing my experiences is more than what was given to me when I first started.

Hopefully, this will help keep you from falling into some of the ditches that I have fallen into. As my husband says, "Eat the meat and spit out the bones." Some of these things may not have happened to you and may never happen to you. This is not a shortcut or a foolproof method for success as a PW. What you put into your role as PW is what you will get out. What I desire to express to you is to be authentic. Be the person who God created you to be, and you'll be the best PW.

God created us as unique individuals to fulfill His intended purpose. Know that His intent from the creation of this world was that you walk as a pastor's wife. It was not an insult or a downgrade, but quite the opposite. You have been uniquely crafted and gifted to fulfill this role from the foundation of the world. Take your role seriously! Love and care for your husband ferociously. Feed His sheep. Take care of His lambs and God will take care of the rest.

Prayer for the pastor's wife

Father God in the name of Jesus, I pray now for the pastor's wife. I thank you, Father, that she is a woman of grace, and her lips are seeded with wisdom. She is strengthened to walk the path You have called her to in this season.

I thank you, Father, that You have called her to dynamic ministry and to do a mighty work with her husband for Your Kingdom in this hour and that they work according to Your vision as two joined, both naturally and spiritually, for Your Glory. I pray that You will cause them to minister effectively to multitudes of Your people in Jesus' name. Father, strengthen them now according to Your perfect will.

I thank you, Father, that she is a faithful member, faithful assistant, and strong ministry partner to her husband, covering him at all times. She will not use her role to undermine or destroy the things You are building. She is a model of submission and power to all of the women in the ministry.

Father, reinforce her marriage so that the rigors of ministry will not shake the foundation that it was built upon. I thank You that You will give them times of restoration and replenishment.

Give her grace, Father God, to not look at the people, but to see wounded and hurting souls in need of restoration. Allow her to see inwardly to the being You created rather than the outward manifestation. Give her the ability to love and minister to your daughters in a way that will be a balm to every wound and bruise they have received. Allow her to be a storehouse to those who are in need and give her the ability to pour richly into them so that they may receive replenishment by Your Grace.

Father, allow her to be a great leader of women with a unique style of leadership organic to her being. Father, allow her to be a deep well of wisdom, virtue, encouragement and love.

I pray for a supernatural unveiling to her right now, in Jesus' name, so that she may view herself as You see her. I praise you, Father, for the mighty woman that she is and that she walks boldly as a pastor's wife. In Jesus' name. Amen.

Devotional for the pastor's wife

I have created these devotionals to highlight traits that will need to increase abundantly in your life as you move forward victoriously as a pastor's wife. There are seven (7) devotionals, one for each day of the week. Use these in your times of prayer and meditation in God's word. Use them as building blocks as I encourage you to scripturally dig deeper into every topic.

Day 1: Submission - Ephesians 5:22-23

Of your many traits as a pastor's wife, your ability to submit is your crowning glory. Married and single women are watching you. Your ability to effectively submit in any situation speaks volumes about your character, your husband's character and the effectiveness of your ministry. Do not underestimate its importance. This is why it is the primary quality for you to possess and hone.

Day 2: Love - 1 Corinthians 13:2

You're going to need an abundance of the ability to love. It makes you more effective in ministry. The love must come from a genuine place as people who you minister to will often quickly sense phony or faked emotions. To love the unlovable, to love those who despitefully use you. To love those who smile in your face and stab you in the back. Ask Jesus to renew and restore your heart.

Day 3: Temperance - Galatians 2:20

It is important that you be able to control yourself: your thoughts, your actions, your speech, and your temper. When you, as a pastor's wife, let the veil of self-control slip, people may see a side of you that they may not like and may lose respect for you. It may be a black mark against the ministry if they are known as having a mean or contentious First Lady. You can be yourself and maintain self-control.

Day 4: Faith - Luke 7:9

We must believe for that which seems impossible. You will be asked to pray for many reasons: for a husband or child, healing, financial matters, employment, restoration, etc. Even when it looks like it's an impossible situation, you will have to speak and move in faith so people will activate their own faith so they can see God move. Without faith, it is impossible to please Him. Your faith will have to extend over your life and each situation like a beacon to guide others who will learn from your example.

Day 5: Wisdom - Proverbs 1:20, James 1:5

As Solomon prayed for wisdom, so should you. The woman in Proverbs 31 moved in wisdom. It should be the fruit of your lips and the leaven to your thoughts. Cultivate wisdom, seek wisdom, and do not stop pursuing the wisdom of God in all things. Women will want to know your thoughts on certain issues concerning their lives. Ask God to seed your lips and thoughts in His Wisdom.

Day 6: Forgiveness - Luke 23:34

Many will offend and hurt. Some arrows are purposely loosed over your life, family, and marriage. Others will lash out in their own anger and hurt. You must forgive. You cannot effectively minister while holding people, places, or things hostage in anger in your heart. You lose your ability to properly represent Jesus if forgiveness is an aspect that you are not liberally applying to every area of your life. Ask God to examine you daily to ensure that you are not harboring unforgiveness.

Day 7: Endurance - 2 Timothy 2:3

God has already equipped you to handle every situation that comes your way. You must endure as a good soldier in Christ Jesus. You must never give up or give in or give place to the enemy. People are counting on you! They are waiting for you to manifest outwardly the things that God has placed on the inside of you. Do not quit! It is not good for man to be alone. You are the support; if you cannot endure, the very foundation may be compromised.

Acknowledgements

I give all glory to God the Father in the name of Jesus, without whom nothing is possible.

To my husband John. I love you. Thank you for your years of encouragement, pushing, pressing, challenging me, and building me up that have turned me into a woman who I no longer recognize. Because of you, I've done things I never thought that I would do; I've been places that I never thought I'd go and experienced things beyond my own imagination. Thank you. I'm the one who murmurs and complains the loudest, yet you always find ways to reign me in and inspire me. All of this is cloaked in your unconditional love. This book would not exist without you. Most certainly it would've never been completed without you.

Much love to my beautiful daughters. Every day, you astound and inspire me. You are three blessings directly from the hand of God. You are amazing, intelligent, and magnificent, each in your own unique way. Never stop being the talented women that the Lord has called you to be. I pray that you will do mighty works for the Kingdom. I hope that seeing your old mom write a book will stir you to do great and wonderful things.

To my family, thank you for your support and encouragement over the years. I appreciate all of the help, support, generosity, babysitting and kind words. I love you all.

To all the members of EFCC, thank you for your support, encouragement and enthusiasm. When I was discouraged, you guys reminded me to get back on track.

Thank you to the Fiverr community especially to the amazing kitd56, who was the best of them all; many thanks to you for helping me over those final hurdles—you are a superstar!

To Prophet Darryl Washington and his lovely wife Prophetess Jackie Washington, thank you!

To Beth Gates, thank you for always listening and for your editorial assistance. Your wit and humor helped me to move forward.

To Pastor Cynthia Monroe Rose, thank you for your kind words, encouragement, and prophetic words that were right on target.

About the author

Elisa Veal lives in Chicago, Illinois, with her husband and three daughters. A pastor's wife since 2002, she was ordained as a pastor in 2013. She loves to bake; some of her recipes have been featured in the magazine *Daughters of A King*. In 2012, she was one of the top 100 home cooks selected to participate on the television show *MasterChef*. She currently serves at Enduring Faith Christian Center where her husband, John Veal, is the Senior Pastor. In her spare time, you will find her reading books or baking batches of delicious desserts. She may be contacted at tobeapw@gmail.com or www.tobeapw.com.

www.ingramcontent.com/pod-product-compliance
Lightning Source LLC
Chambersburg PA
CBHW031551040426
42452CB00006B/266